Principles of Research Design in the Social Sciences

Frank Bechhofer and
Lindsay Paterson

London and New York

First published 2000
by Routledge
11 New Fetter Lane, London EC4P 4EE

Simultaneously published in the USA and Canada
by Routledge
29 West 35th Street, New York, NY 10001

Routledge is an imprint of the Taylor & Francis Group

© 2000 Frank Bechhofer and Lindsay Paterson

Typeset in Goudy by Taylor & Francis Books Ltd
Printed and bound in Great Britain by MPG Books Ltd, Bodmin

British Library Cataloguing in Publication Data
A catalogue record for this book is available from the British Library

Library of Congress Cataloging in Publication Data
Principles of research design in the social sciences / Frank
Bechhofer and Lindsay Paterson.
　Includes bibliographical references.
　1. Social sciences – Research.　2. Social sciences – Methodology.
　I. Paterson, Lindsay.　II. Title.
　H61.B425　2000　99–44348
　300' .7'2–dc21　CIP

ISBN 0–415–21442–4 (hbk)
ISBN 0–415–21443–2 (pbk)

Principles of Research Design in the Social Sciences

Principles of Research Design in the Social Sciences is a book for researchers who know what they want to study, but who have yet to decide how best to study it. This book does not aim to provide a set of rigid recipes for social scientists – like many methodology books do – rather it is intended to stimulate them to think about the issues involved when deciding upon their research design.

By discussing standard approaches to research design and method in various disciplines within the social sciences, the authors illustrate why particular designs have traditionally predominated in certain areas of study. But whilst they acknowledge the strengths of these standard approaches, Bechhofer and Paterson's emphasis is on helping researchers to find the most effective solution to their given problem, encouraging them, through this familiarity with the principles of a variety of approaches, to innovate where appropriate.

Principles of Research Design in the Social Sciences will prove indispensable to students of all levels in the social sciences embarking upon a research project, and to experienced researchers looking for a fresh perspective on their object of study.

Frank Bechhofer is Professor at the Research Centre for Social Sciences at the University of Edinburgh. **Lindsay Paterson** is Professor in the Faculty of Education at the University of Edinburgh.

Social Research Today
Series editor: Martin Bulmer

Related titles:

Contents

Preface

If you want to plan a piece of empirical social research, you have to make decisions about how the research is to be carried out. You have to choose a set of procedures which enable your aims and objectives to be realised in practice. The aim of this book is to help you to do that – not by providing a set of recipes, but by stimulating you to think about the issues involved in choosing a research design. So the book is written mainly for social scientists who have done little research before, who already have a broad idea of what they want to study, but who are just beginning to work out how to study it.

The organising principles we use are comparison and control. We argue in Chapter 1 that these ideas are fundamental to research design, and in each of the later chapters – devoted to particular ways of going about a research project – we consider the different roles of comparison and control in different types of research. The book itself is informed by comparison. At several places, we compare different designs, and we would encourage you to read through the whole text, even though you may be fairly sure you know what design you want to use: in order to be clear about the effectiveness of the design you have chosen, you should know why you are not using certain others.

One reason for this is that it is easy to restrict yourself unthinkingly to the standard repertoire of designs in the main academic discipline to which you are attached. So, if you are a psychologist you might tend to use experiments or observation. If you are a sociologist or political scientist, you might incline towards surveys or interviews. If you are an anthropologist, you would be most likely to think first about fieldwork and participant observation. And if you work in one of the many professional social disciplines – such as education, social work, criminology or social medicine – you are likely to favour a fairly eclectic mixture of surveys, interviews, case studies and observation.

There are good reasons, especially historically, why these various disciplines have evolved the preferences they have. Experiments predominate in psychology because it has had strong links with the biological sciences. Sociology and politics initially preferred social surveys because they wanted to study whole societies, and then in these disciplines there was a reaction against that towards smaller-scale work that was more interested in respondents' meanings than in statistical categorisation. Anthropology started as the study of cultures that were wholly unfamiliar to the researcher, and so seemed to require immersion to get anywhere at all. And the areas of professional study – like most policy research – drew on several disciplines, and so drew designs and methods from each of them. The book discusses these standard approaches in the separate disciplines, and illustrates their effectiveness by numerous examples of successful research.

But you do not have to restrict yourself to the standard approaches. The very fact that policy research, for example, has successfully used a variety of designs should encourage all social scientists to be innovative where appropriate. The important question is whether the design you have chosen is adequate to handle your research problem. As well as thinking about well-known designs from other disciplines, you should also be open to using quite novel ways of collecting data. We encourage that approach throughout the book, and – in Chapter 10 – discuss explicitly some sources which are often ignored by social scientists.

The book is about design, not about how to do the research after a design is chosen. But to choose a design, you have to know something of what it entails. Put differently: how a set of data was gathered will circumscribe the methods which can be used to analyse it. You can no more apply statistical modelling to observational data than you can use social surveys to investigate, say, the psychology of inter-personal relationships. More specifically, the type of statistical modelling you use will depend on whether you have conducted a survey or an experiment, and on whether you have followed up your initial contact with respondents to see how they have changed. Likewise, what your analysis can make of a transcript of an interview will depend on whether it was formal or informal, whether you and the interviewee were alone together or were part of a social group, and – again – whether the interview was part of a series with the same person.

Thus there is really no clear boundary between design and methods: choosing a design involves also choosing a method (or at most a restricted set of methods), and so the implications of particular methods have to be understood before a study is designed. This requires you to develop some understanding of the philosophical principles that allow various methods to be valuable. The book tries to provide this: we believe that the important points about the common methods in social research can be grasped in sufficient depth to allow a choice among the designs that lead to these methods to be made in a reasonably well-informed way.

The book presents ideas, not technicalities. Choosing a design for a piece of social science research involves knowing about the strengths and weaknesses of different approaches. But that choice does not usually require a technical knowledge of all types of design and method: what matters are the principles which underpin them. This book presents these principles, and compares them with each other. It is not a toolkit: it does not show you how to conduct a survey, nor how to carry out an interview. It does assess the principles involved in opting for any of the main ways of doing research in the social sciences, and therefore allows rational choices to be made among these techniques by people who have to choose. It aims, therefore, to stimulate reflection and further thought. On the other hand, the book is close to the practice of research in that it discusses the principles in the light of their consequences for doing the research. The book attempts to be well informed and rigorous from a philosophical point of view, but is also empirically grounded in the practical needs of researchers.

On the same principle of being concerned with ideas, not technicalities, the main text is not heavily burdened with bibliographic references: references here are confined to specific quotations and empirical illustrations. Suggestions for further reading are in a bibliographic essay, but it, too, does not attempt to be a comprehensive bibliography – merely an indication of how to take further the ideas and examples in the main text.

Research design as we discuss it in this book is neither deeply complex (like some aspects of philosophy, theory or, say, statistical modelling over time) nor is it an arcane topic. The issues we discuss are very practical, and the focus is on how to achieve the research goals you set yourself. On the other hand, it is easy to be misled into thinking that research design is simple. The process of research design requires the researcher to develop habits of innovative and lateral thinking; the best designs often require great imagination, invention and a willingness, in principle at least, to avoid the obvious. In doing so, the whole enterprise of doing research becomes much more satisfying intellectually.

Acknowledgements

We are grateful to Ashgate Publishing for permission to reproduce Figures 6.1 and 6.3, and to Penguin UK for permission to use the extracts from Rosemary Edmonds's translation of *War and Peace* in Chapter 10. We are grateful to David McCrone for reading the whole text of a draft of the book and making many insightful comments. We are also grateful to Richard B. Davies, Pamela Munn, Maria Scott and David Smith for commenting on the general ideas in the book and on drafts of Chapters 1 and 3. Many of the ideas were also refined through being used with classes for postgraduate research students in the Faculties of Social Science and of Education at the University of Edinburgh. The responsibility for the final version is, of course, our own. The book is a collaborative work to which each author contributed equally: the order of names on the title page reflects only the alphabet.

1 Fundamentals
Comparison and control

In this chapter, we set the scene by explaining why we see the two concepts of comparison and control as so central to research design that focusing on them allows us to make judgements about the strengths and weaknesses of various approaches to research. We shall start by locating the two concepts in the research process, and then discuss each of them in turn in greater detail.

Comparison and control in the research process

Despite the steady growth in social research over the last forty to fifty years, it is quite easy for social scientists to think of many topics about which we know rather little, social problems which we would like to solve, and explanations for social phenomena which are less than satisfactory. Anyone wishing to embark on research is likely to have an adequate knowledge of the literature and the necessary intellectual curiosity about the social world around them to be able to do this.

Ideas for a research project can be generated in ways which correspond to those three categories, which are intended to be illustrative rather than exhaustive. The discovery of a hitherto insufficiently explored area often coincides with economic, political or social changes which make it topical. An example is the explosion in research on small businesses in the 1980s. What is regarded as a social problem at any moment in time may be primarily a matter of perception or moral panic. For instance, fear of crime does not by any means always correspond to its severity or incidence and why this should be so is an interesting research question (see for example Hough 1995). Nevertheless, AIDS prevention, the incidence of drug taking or alcoholism, the impact of unemployment, or variations in educational provision might all be seen by various social scientists as social problems worthy of further attention. A wish to improve on or offer a drastically different explanation of some social phenomenon which is dominant in the literature is a powerful driver of research activity.

Undoubtedly some people find it easier than others to generate a project in these general terms, and to some extent it is a learned capacity. Researchers need to develop an eye for events, patterns and groups of people which are in some way anomalous and do not fit accepted theories and arguments, and to learn the habit of questioning the taken-for-granted. Such variations in ability are inevitable in research as in other areas of life, but it is in our experience unusual for anyone to embark on a research career or work for a higher degree without some idea of what it is they wish to study, at least in general and sometimes rather vague terms.

What is often less appreciated is that while it is relatively easy to generate a research problem, working out how to actually do the research, that is, settling on an adequate research design, is much less straightforward. As a counsel of excellence, what all researchers ought to aim at is the kind of research design which, once articulated, seems so attractive and obvious as to lead others to say 'I wish I had thought of that!'. What is it then about some research designs which makes them so convincing?

It is the fundamental contention of this book that a good research design can be judged by the way it approaches the two issues of comparison and control. Designing a piece of empirical research requires the researcher to decide on the best ways of collecting data in research locales which will permit meaningful and insightful comparisons. At the same time the research design must achieve the control which gives some degree of certainty that the explanations offered are indeed superior to competing explanations. Control for us is an epistemological concept, not an organisational one. Concern with control does not imply that one wishes or indeed is able to manipulate the situation, and the need to achieve control applies as much to the most natural and participatory fieldwork situations as to experimental ones. Research designs will differ greatly in terms of the place or places where the research is carried out, the methods used to gather data and the analytic techniques used. Control can be achieved in different ways at each of these stages, and it is for this reason that the chapters of this book deal not only with what are self-evidently design issues, such as the use of experiments or sampling, but also the implications for comparison and control of using interviews or fieldwork as part of a design.

In principle, making the right comparisons and being reasonably sure that the conclusions drawn are sound may seem an obvious goal of research, regardless of how difficult it may be in practice. Readers who come from some disciplines, psychology for example, may marvel that we find it necessary to foreground comparison and control as a connecting thread through the entire book. It is worth considering for a moment why this should be so. For those trained as undergraduates in certain disciplines, especially those where experimentation is paradigmatic, these ideas are so deeply embedded as to be self-evidently the foundations of empirical enquiry. Concepts and theories are intertwined with empirical findings and, crucially, with the procedures leading to these findings.

Within disciplines, departments do of course vary greatly in their approach, and we do not wish to over-generalise. Nevertheless, in other areas of social science, such as politics, sociology or social policy, the emphasis in methods courses is often on specific techniques such as the interview or surveys. There may also be a heavy emphasis on the philosophical underpinnings of the discipline and the place of empirical enquiry within it. Where this is the case, there is often very much less emphasis on comparison and control at an undergraduate level, and this difference is interesting in itself. People who are trained in one way come to think almost automatically about comparison and ideas of control, especially experimental control, as a result of the way in which they are taught. In much the same way, many natural scientists are taught implicitly about the ways in which research is done and the design of experiments, without great emphasis being placed on this. It is absorbed from very early on, from schooldays indeed, as the way in which science is done. The methods and techniques of natural science are deeply embedded in natural scientific knowledge itself; the ways in which the knowledge was obtained are part of the knowledge claims themselves.

In many undergraduate courses in social sciences, the acquisition of the necessary knowledge and skills to carry out research is separated artificially from the process of learning the substantive content of the discipline. The widespread existence of courses on research methods is testament to this, and while courses on theoretical issues or substantive areas of a discipline *may* treat the ways in which empirical enquiry proceeds as intrinsic to the knowledge being discussed, this is by no means the rule. Thus research methods are very often seen as distinct from the knowledge they aim to develop; sometimes the distinction becomes a deep gulf. For the many researchers initially trained in this way, the idea that comparison and control are the basic building blocks of research design will be much less familiar, and our emphasis on the inseparability of theory, concept and method may even seem novel.

Comparison

In our view, then, knowledge in social science is built on implicit or explicit comparisons. Comparison is a fundamental aspect of cognition, and much research procedure codifies and formalises that cognitive process. It is arguable that much everyday behaviour is itself based on such comparisons, and it is this parallel which we want to explore first.

A possible model of human behaviour is predicated on the idea of individuals making choices, and some social scientists would wish to extend this to collectivities making choices, arguing that this should be seen as distinct from, even if based upon, the choices of individuals within those collectivities (see the discussion in Coleman 1990). Different disciplines would vary in their assumptions about and emphasis on the kinds and extent of constraints which affect these choices, but would share the notion that such choices are made. The choices are among options and, in order to make the choices, individuals and collectivities have to compare these options in a more or less formal way. We cite this simply to show how innate comparison is, and how little we normally think about or realise that we are making comparisons. Thus we make choices among options continually and almost automatically in everyday life, evaluating the options in various ways by comparison.

Some very fundamental aspects of behaviour have this element. For example, in everyday life comparison is the basis of sexism or racism, because the systematic degrading of one sex or of other races is based on a belief of superiority which demands the making of a comparison. Our sense of national identity is predicated on comparison; those who see themselves as Scottish generally do so by comparison with the English. Those who see themselves as predominantly English or Scottish do so in contradistinction to claiming a British identity. In the world of research, when we investigate equal opportunity, we systematically compare sexes, classes, races or national groups with regard to some outcome such as income or unemployment, health, or access to further and higher education.

Now, there is no absolute reason why the underpinnings of social science research design should mirror or be isomorphic with social behaviour, but it is arguable at least that, as the carrying-out of research is itself a form of social behaviour, this is likely to be so. Underlying this rather simple idea are much deeper concerns which we shall touch on from time to time in this book. The reflexivity of social research, the way in which the process of carrying out a research project on social life is itself part of that social life, has given rise to a vast literature. The belief that research in social science is in no important way different from research by physical scientists into the natural world was never as widespread as some claim, but the general acceptance of the need to take very seriously the issues raised by reflexivity has profoundly affected the way research methods and findings are regarded. The pendulum has now perhaps swung too far in the other direction, so that it is necessary for us to state that we remain unrepentantly of the view that empirical enquiry based on comparison which also attempts to maximise control is fundamental to social science. In other words, it is possible through comparison and control to acquire relatively objective knowledge about the social world.

Sometimes people talk about description in a manner which suggests that one can describe absolutely, so that what is observed and described relates only to that which is being described; no comparison is involved. We would reject this view. The act of description requires one explicitly or implicitly to compare the object being described with something else, and it is this feature which makes the idea of 'pure description' meaningless. When the comparison is implicit, it is easy to be misled into believing that it is not being made at all. As a result, the view is sometimes expressed that description is easy and should form no part of serious social research. The phrase 'mere description', occasionally used when referring to ethnography for instance, makes clear the derogatory intent. On closer examination, all description is both comparative and theory-laden because in describing we choose what to describe. No social situation or behaviour can be described exhaustively. We must always select from a potentially infinite wealth of possible observations, and in making them we implicitly compare what we see with something else. Good research design requires social scientists to make those selections in a conceptually informed way and their comparisons explicit.

It is relatively straightforward to show the implicit process in action. If, for example, one asks a number of people to go to a busy road junction and for a period of half an hour to observe and write down what they see, the results are illuminating. What happens is that in order to cope with the task, each individual observer has to make a series of decisions about what it would be interesting, or straightforward, or valuable to record, and in this way they make the problem manageable by selecting a sample from the vast population of possible observations. Clearly, there are far more things to observe at a busy traffic junction than any one individual could possibly handle, and so some sorts of criteria for selection have to be used. They may be systematic or *ad hoc*; conscious and explicit or simply taken for granted. The process is implicitly theory-laden in that we select what to observe according to what we believe is relevant to our goal of understanding what is happening. This theory may be incomplete or very crude. If the persons carrying out this exercise are social scientists, one would expect, or at least hope, that the observations would be more systematic, explicitly guided by some kind of theoretical or conceptual framework which seeks to explain the phenomena they are observing.

The social scientific obligation to select in some fairly systematic, that is, theory-laden, manner can be deferred but not avoided by the use of technology. For instance, it would be possible to film the events at this road junction, although to obtain an even nearly complete record is considerably more difficult than one might imagine. The images which have been recorded can subsequently be analysed in the office or the laboratory. Filming first and then analysing the data does not, however, fundamentally alter the underlying process. What it does is to allow the researcher to take the necessary sample of observations at leisure, possibly playing and replaying the film to make this possible. In this way, observation can be made much more systematic, following closely laid down rules of selection and classification, thus making the relationship between theory and observation more explicit. However it is to be done, the fundamental point remains that all description involves a comparison of the object described with something else. Social scientists usually compare observations grouped according to some explicit classification, which in turn depends on having a degree of conceptual understanding. We might, for instance, be interested in driver behaviour and have some *a priori* classification of 'good' or 'bad' behaviour. What was understood by 'good' or 'bad' would be affected by our conceptual approach. If our model of driver behaviour was derived from an understanding of 'safe' driving we would classify events in one way. If we were concerned with 'technically skilful' driving, the classification rules might be rather different.

Comparison is, then, unavoidable in social science. If knowledge is to be systematically advanced, the choice of what is to be compared with what should depend explicitly on theoretical perspective. A rather nice and well-known example is the use of absolute and relative measures of poverty. As long ago as 1901, Rowntree first attempted to assess the extent of poverty in Britain. He used an absolute measure whereby he laid down the criteria for a basket of goods required to keep the person at a minimum standard of living, and then tried to assess what proportion of the population were living above and below this standard.

Over half a century later, Runciman in 1966 produced his celebrated book, *Relative Deprivation and Social Justice*. The underlying idea was that it was not the absolute conditions or condition in which someone lived which was the central issue in stratification and perceptions of social justice, but the reference group with whom they compared themselves. Deprivation was relative, and people assessed their situation by comparing their situation with others. Thus, for example, a group of manual workers might compare themselves with another manual group, or perhaps with industrial white-collar workers or with professionals such as doctors. In assessing their earnings, standard of living or quality of life, they would compare themselves with their chosen reference group. Now, they may have had imperfect information, and their comparison may have been in some absolute sense incorrect, but nonetheless the important issue in Runciman's view was the perceived degree of relative deprivation, with the stress on relative as opposed to absolute.

By 1979, we find in a classic modern survey of poverty in the United Kingdom (Townsend 1979) that the idea of poverty Townsend was using was no longer Rowntree's absolute measure but one of *relative* poverty. That is to say, poverty must be viewed in relation to the standard of living of the population as a whole, and the expectations which individuals and families have when they view their situation in comparison to others. Thus Townsend defined poverty as a proportion of the median wage or income in the society. If poverty is viewed conceptually in this way, then someone who would have been rated by Rowntree as well above the poverty line, not in danger of starvation, minimally housed and able to keep warm and dry, will nevertheless be seen as poor in today's society.

How we define and measure poverty is, then, closely related to the kind of explanations we are developing and the theory underlying them. As in many areas of social science, the political environment plays a role here and is theorised in the sense that these different approaches are pred-icated on different assumptions, including political ones. This is evident in more recent debates about the measurement of poverty, including attempts, by commentators from right across the political spectrum, to replicate the Rowntree basket-of-goods approach (see for instance Stitt and Grant 1993; Stitt 1994; Pryke 1995). However, many of the things we now regard as essential would have seemed luxurious in Rowntree's day. Even those hostile to the poor consider that the ownership of some of these possessions or living in a particular way is an intrinsic part of not being in poverty. So even unsympathetic observers would accept as poverty-stricken a higher standard of living than would have been the case in 1901. Thus one can think of poverty as being relative in two ways, along two dimensions, to use a familiar spatial metaphor. First of all in the sense that it changes over time as the society as a whole changes, and second, in some conceptualisations, that the measurement of poverty has to be by comparison with other citizens of the same society, or possibly of other societies.

Comparison is an inescapable element of research design, and where theory is reasonably well developed it is the researcher's theoretical frame-work which shapes the comparisons. Comparison and control are directed towards the testing and refinement of well-articulated ideas about the social phenomena in question. These ideas need to be sufficiently sharply specified to allow the researcher, on the basis of the empirical findings, to decide whether to take them forward, albeit usually in a modified or developed form, or to reject them and seek an alternative explanation. Often, however, good explanations are thin on the ground and theory generation is the prime goal of a particular piece of research. Here again we would argue that comparison is central to the endeavour.

This underlies the well-known idea of grounded theory as first discussed by Glaser and Strauss in 1967, which embeds the idea of comparison into theory generation. *The Discovery of Grounded Theory* by Glaser and Strauss has been enormously influential, partly because the empirical work done by these authors, singly and together, is of an exceptionally high standard. The idea of grounded theory and the research procedures associated with it have been accepted into the general body of thinking in many social sciences, and are frequently referred to. Admittedly, a sceptic might form the opinion that these references are sometimes ritual rather than based on a careful reading of the original work and understanding of the original idea, but the notion of grounded theory and the kind of procedures which Glaser and Strauss advocate are well worth considering. It was a fundamental contention of their book that social science at the time was overly concerned with the *testing* of theories generated *a priori* and inadequately concerned with theory *generation*. It is debatable whether social science in the 1950s and 1960s was ever as dominated by the testing of theories of this kind as Glaser and Strauss imply. Certainly, some social science disciplines did follow a theory testing approach, but in others it might be argued that theory was regrettably never sufficiently developed, whether *a priori* or from imaginative enquiry, to allow for adequate testing. Other social scientists reject theory testing on philosophical grounds.

Clearly, our previously stated view, that a research design must achieve the control which gives some degree of certainty that explanations offered are indeed superior to competing explanations, is entirely compatible with the generation of those explanations *a priori* from a body of well-developed theory where this is possible.

On the other hand, because, across many areas of social science, theory is not well developed, we see the generation of adequate theory as an important goal. For us, then, one of the ways in which Glaser and Strauss suggested that theory could best be generated is especially significant. This approach employs the continual and imaginative use of comparison. Much oversimplified, their underlying idea was that empirical situations should be compared not in order to see whether the theory held or not, but in order to develop it and elaborate it. The target of their criticisms was that version of the classic model of research whereby hypotheses developed from a theory are tested and re-tested by a repeated series of similar experiments or enquiries. For Glaser and Strauss, this extensive repetition was inefficient and unnecessary. The social scientist should instead see whether the conclusion reached held under contrasting but conceptually related circumstances. Social science should rely on imaginative comparison rather than replication. Thus they suggest that a researcher, having formed a series of ideas about a particular organisation, shall we say the emergency ward of a hospital, should not replicate these findings by going into another emergency ward and seeing whether the same conceptual framework again explained what was going on there, but should seek an empirically apparently contrasting situation which might nonetheless be conceptually similar. Thus, in the case of emergency wards, they suggested that fire departments might be an interesting field-work locale. The imaginative extension and refinement of a theory by continuously comparing its applicability in contrasting situations until further refinement is unnecessary is seen as the ideal research design.

In order to avoid confusion, it must be understood that we have here focused on only one specific aspect of grounded theory: the choice of contrasting situations in which to pursue the extension and improvement of a theory. It is important to make this point, if only to avoid being drawn into a fierce but also illuminating controversy which has arisen between the originators of grounded theory. The interested reader will find a summary and the relevant references in Melia (1996).

Control

A good research design is one which gives the researcher confidence in the solidity of the conclusions drawn from the data. Achieving this requires a high degree of control. This statement of the ideal is simple to state and, up to a point, to grasp. The ideas which lie behind it are complex and sometimes contested. Achieving it not only requires knowledge, thought and ingenuity, but a realisation that research design inevitably involves compromises because it is impossible to maximise everything which is desirable.

The basic issue is most easily approached within a causal framework, although we accept readily that not all social scientists are happy with the ideas of cause or causal methodology. Let us start with an apparently trivial medical example. Suppose someone tells us that on a sequence of ten very bright sunny days they got a headache every day. We might decide to think about this, to speculate a little. Let us imagine first that we then note that on the next five days which are not bright and sunny they also get a headache every day. To relate back to the earlier discussion, we are making a guided comparison here. When we make this comparison and reflect on it, we would probably conclude with some confidence that bright sun had nothing to do with the problem. In a real example, there would perhaps be a probabilistic element. The subject might have got a headache on nine of the ten bright days and also on four of the five dull days. We would again probably decide that it was reasonably certain that sunlight was not causally involved.

Now suppose that the outcomes are different, and that on dull days all is well and the sufferer is free from headaches. We might then conclude that sunshine does indeed seem to be associated with these headaches. Being duly cautious about the distinction between association and cause we might tentatively infer that it was causally involved. Again, in practice, the person might get a headache on nine rather than ten of the sunny days and only be free of headache on four of the five dull days. If, as is compatible with experience and other information, we accept that the sunlight may be a trigger but not an absolutely inevitable trigger of a headache, and also that there are many causes of headaches, we might again decide that it was reasonably certain that sunlight was involved in this person's headaches. Whether this conclusion would apply more generally is of course another matter.

We shall return to the discussion of cause in Chapter 2, but it is easy to see in this example how theory is involved. Bright sunlight and glare cause people to screw up their eyes, and even a lay knowledge tells us that this might give one a headache. Even this apparently simple example, however, is more complicated than it seems at first glance. To anticipate a little the later discussion, if we wanted to increase our confidence in our conclusions we would have to take into account some alternative explanations. After making the first set of observations, we would have to consider the possibility that the headaches experienced in the first ten days were indeed caused by the bright sunlight and those on the subsequent five dull days by something quite other. Simply stating it in that way makes us feel intuitively that it is not likely that this is really what happened but we have to take the possibility seriously, and thus avoid drawing a quite erroneous conclusion. Similarly, when evaluating the second set of observations, we have to consider that the headache on the bright days might have been caused by something quite other than the glare, and that whatever it was that caused it was for some reason not operative on the five dull days.

Control is about manipulating the research design, or the analysis, or both, to raise as far as is possible the probability that we really are sure about the conclusion to which we are coming. In our trivial example, we might manipulate the situation by suggesting that the subject try wearing dark glasses on sunny days. If, most of the time, the person then did not get headaches, our belief in our conclusion that the sunlight was in some way responsible would become stronger. If dark glasses made no difference, we would become more sceptical about our initial conclusions. Generally in social science we cannot manipulate the situation quite so easily, and we may not be able to speculate about the cause or links quite so readily. But if we can control the situation experimentally, we can to some extent exclude alternative false explanations.

Very often in social science, however, we cannot control the situation experimentally and have to obtain control mainly at the analysis stage. When, for instance, we analyse survey data, it is much more difficult to exclude the possibility that other factors may be at work leading us to a false cause or conclusion. Probably the most famous example in the methodological literature comes from the writings of Paul Lazarsfeld, who pointed out that lots of fire engines attending a fire raise the cost of the damage. Experimentation is not feasible; varying the number of fire engines sent to a fire in some systematic way would not be permitted or morally acceptable. Now, it is fairly easy to see that in this example it seems unlikely that the fire engines are actually *causing* the bulk of the damage. Obviously, what is happening is that both the extent of the damage and the arrival of lots of fire engines are determined by the size of the fire. Extent of damage and the number of fire engines are certainly associated, but they are both caused by a third variable, the extent of the fire.

There is a charming illustration from Central Europe of these difficulties of drawing causal comparisons. One used to be able to observe there that large numbers of storks in an area were associated with a high birth rate, which might lead one to believe that a traditional theory of family building was in fact correct. Sadly for lovers of folk myth, once again the reality is similar to the fire engines example. In rural areas there tended to be a higher birth rate at that time due to causes quite other than storks, and rural areas also had far more storks than urban ones.

Essentially, in survey analysis we attempt to achieve control *post hoc* by manipulating the variables available to us at the analysis stage. If we are fortunate enough to have very large samples, high response rates, excellent questionnaires which successfully anticipate the variables which will be needed in the analysis, and high-quality data collection, we can achieve high levels of control by employing extremely careful analysis. Control is further enhanced, at the cost of statistical complexity, if we can gather data over time (see Chapter 8). Modern survey analysis has reached a high level of intellectual and statistical sophistication, but much survey research inevitably involves difficult compromises. Even in professional full-time research there will very rarely, if ever, be enough time and money, which are closely interlinked, to maximise all the desir-able characteristics just listed. Most surveys carried out by students are likely to be relatively small-scale, limited and exploratory, requiring great caution when drawing conclusions. Where a survey forms part or all of a research design, its strengths always have to be balanced against its limita-tions. Secondary survey analysis, where already existing survey data are used, may offer relatively easy and cheap access to large, well-drawn samples of data collected in a highly professional manner. The variables collected may not be exactly what one would wish, so that again there has to be a compromise. With ingenuity it may be possible to design a very strong piece of research using secondary analysis, accepting that there are always trade-offs in research, and a gain in control in one regard has to be balanced against a loss in another.

Control in the sense in which we are using the word is no less critical in qualitative research, but here the approach has to be somewhat different. We shall discuss the issue in greater detail in Chapter 5 and especially in Chapter 7, but one standard technique is to search systemati-cally for instances which run against the understanding one is developing. This can be done very effectively in the process of fieldwork, where it is analogous to manipulating variables in an experiment (for an early and celebrated example see Becker's study of medical students (1961), discussed further in McCall and Simmons 1969: 245–57). Just as one can to a degree achieve control *post hoc* in the survey, one can search *post hoc* for counter-instances in fieldwork notes or transcribed interviews, accepting that the data set is now a given entity, fixed by the procedures and research design by which one collected them. It is interesting that just as secondary analysis of survey data has been greatly advanced by the increasing size, quality and use of survey archives such as the ESRC Data Archive at the University of Essex, archives of qualitative data are being slowly assembled with a view to secondary analysis. The problems of confidentiality, ethics and interpretation are immense, but progress is being made.

There are, then, many ways of introducing control into a research design, some more effective than others. Standards of control are gener-ally assessed against one classic exemplar – the experiment. To design a good experiment means having a really well-grounded understanding of what may threaten the soundness of our conclusions. We tend to think of experiments as relatively small-scale, carried out in the laboratory or perhaps the classroom. They have been carried out on a somewhat larger scale, for instance in industrial settings like the so-called Hawthorne experiments which we touch on in Chapter 2, and experimentation as we normally think of it shades into evaluation where different interventions into social processes are evaluated to compare, or more often determine, their effectiveness. We discuss this further and give a number of examples in Chapter 9, which deals with policy research. These interventions on a fairly grand scale are certainly experiments in that some variable is manipulated to see what effect this has on some measured outcome, be it crime reduction, re-offending, health promotion or early learning. The aim is to use our understanding of the process as reflected in established theory to control those variables which we expect might affect the outcome. In these large-scale natural experiments, controlling factors other than the main experimental variable may be impossible without unacceptable intrusion into people's private lives; even the initial intervention may be difficult to justify.

Experimental designs, especially on a small scale under highly manipulable conditions, can enable research to achieve very high levels of control, at the cost of considerable complexity and a degree of artificiality which has often been criticised. In fact, such complex experimental designs can rarely be achieved in social science outside of psychology, although some experimental work has been done in economics. However, it is the contention of this book that a really good understanding of comparison and of control is what is needed if one is to create good research designs. And one way of approaching the question of how to set up a good research design which achieves control is to treat the controlled experiment as some kind of gold standard, a model against which we can evaluate other research designs. That is one reason why the next chapter examines the principles underlying experimental design.

2   Experiments

Experiments are not so common in social research as are most of the other designs we discuss in this book. They are extensively used in the various branches of psychology, in areas of economics, in the social branches of medicine and in some types of policy evaluation; but they are uncommon in sociology, politics and anthropology. Nevertheless, despite this patchiness in popularity, there are still good reasons to think about experiments, not just because they are very important in fields such as psychology, but also because the reasons why most social scientists do not do experiments are themselves quite interesting, and quite revealing about the approaches which are more widely used.

The first reason for looking at experiments does offer genuinely wider lessons. When we are thinking through what we can say with the research designs that we are actually using, it is important always to think about what we cannot say. Indeed, doing that is part of the educational philosophy that runs through this entire book: it is why we cover nine different types of approach to research, and suggest that, no matter what the design might be that is appropriate to any particular project, the researcher always has to be clear why other methods have been rejected.

The second reason to know about experiments is that, according to a certain view of social science research – which we do not share – everything we do is merely a rather inadequate approximation to the ideal circumstance of an experiment. For example, one writer has this to say about how to interpret educational research:

> The solution [to the problem of interpretation] adopted in medicine is the clinical trial or randomised experiment. In social science we shall have to use the same approach if we want to obtain clear evidence of the effects of various [policy] programmes.
>
> (Fitz-Gibbon 1988: 94)

So, from this perspective, the model against which the design of any social science is compared is the randomised experiment. For example, if we are interested in understanding the effects of unemployment on individuals, the argument would be that the standard against which any research is compared is an imaginary experiment in which people were randomly allocated to being unemployed. The alleged problem with other ways of doing such research would be that people who happen to be unemployed also have all sorts of other personal and social characteristics, the effects of which cannot be separated from the effects of unemployment as such.

In this chapter, once we have looked in more detail at why the randomised experiment has seemed to be such an attractive model for research, we will be asking whether, for most social investigation, it is a relevant model at all.

There are three sections in this chapter:

- We start by giving some examples to illustrate what experiments can do in social science research.
- Then we draw out from these examples some of the general principles that underlie the use of experiments, and we discuss, from these general principles, the scope for implementing experiments with human populations. The crucial thing about an experiment is intervention, a term we have borrowed from Hacking (1983). Experimenters deliberately intervene to investigate a cause; in other words, they apply something that is called a treatment and try to hold everything else constant so as to get control.
- Having concluded from that section that there is actually quite limited scope for using experiments with human beings, in the third part we talk about types of experiment, sometimes called quasi-experiments, that are more widely used in social sciences.

What are experiments?

The first example is a very simple one, although it is quite close in structure to many real experiments that have been done in education. Imagine that we wanted to test a new method of teaching spelling to primary school children. As a very simple design for this experiment, we would take a class of children and divide it in half; one half of the class would be taught by the new method and the other half by a method with which we want to compare it, often called the 'control'. And then at the end of a period of time, say a year or six months, we would give the class some sort of test. On the basis of the results in that test, we would assess whether the new method had been more effective than the control. There are refinements of this which we will come to shortly, but that is the essence of an experiment – that we intervene to change something, in this case the method of teaching. In the language associated with experiments, the things we are interested in – here the teaching methods – are often called the 'treatments'.

One thing that is often thought of as being part of an experiment is 'random allocation'. The two different halves of the class in the example are chosen at random. There are many mechanisms for doing that, usually nowadays by computer. In our example, one simple way would be by tossing a coin. So if there are thirty children in the class, you would toss a coin for each of them and if it comes up heads then that child gets taught the new method and if it is tails then the child is taught by the old method.

The mechanisms for random allocation, or 'randomisation' as it is often called, are unimportant. What does matter is the epistemological role that randomisation is supposed to play. In the literature on experiments, there is a great deal of confusion about this. The first purpose that is often thought of as being the role of randomisation is one that is very widely recognised. The idea is that, on average in some sense, the two groups of pupils will be identical if they are randomly assigned to these two different methods of teaching. So, for example, it may be that in one particular experiment you could have a slight imbalance of boys and girls. You could easily end up with nine boys and six girls getting the new method, and therefore six boys and nine girls getting the other one. The argument is that we should not be worried about that because, if we did this experiment over and over again, each time randomly allocating pupils to the teaching method, we would get it balancing out. On average, there would be the same proportion of boys and girls getting the new method as getting the control. And, similarly, there would be balance with respect to every other characteristic of a pupil that we might care to consider – their exact age or their height or their eye colour or their shoe size or their parental background. There would be, on average, balance with respect to all the irrelevant things as well as the relevant ones.

This first role for randomisation divides into two versions. One version is straightforward and the other is more problematic. If we have very large numbers participating in our experiment – if instead of just thirty people in one class we had 3,000 people in many classes – then, of course, if you randomly allocated each one to new or control, you would indeed be very close to an exact balance of male and female within each method. You might get 746 boys and 754 girls, say, in one particular method, but the imbalance would be no more than slight because the numbers would be so large. But that type of argument does not work in smaller examples, such as the one with just thirty pupils, where there is very likely to be a substantial imbalance.

It is at this point, for small experiments, that the second version of this first role of randomisation comes in. We imagine repeating the experiment many times, and refer to balance on average over all the repetitions. Why do we talk about this imaginary repetition of the same experiment? Hacking (1983) argues that it is based ultimately on some imagined community of rational investigators all attempting the same experiment and sharing the results. When we are doing this experiment, we have to imagine what the ideal type of rational human being would do in similar circumstances. Amongst a hypothetically infinite collection of similar experiments, half of the control group will be female and half of the new treatment group will be female.

So in the case of the small numbers, the argument for random allocation is that it is the most objective way of doing it. It is what any rational human being would do in similar circumstances. As Hacking points out, that concept of a rational human being is itself an ideological construct, a common project of rational investigation that we are all engaged in as social scientists. But if we accept that part of the argument, then it does not seem unreasonable to adopt a mechanism that would be persuasive to similar types of people doing similar kinds of things in similar circumstances. So that is why, even in the case where there is not going to be an exact balance of male and female or any other characteristic in the particular small group of people whom you are studying, it might nevertheless be rational to do the random allocation.

That is the first role of random allocation. It says that, on average, the two groups would be balanced with respect to any characteristics that you might imagine. The reason why you would want them to be balanced is that you do not want the results to be confused by extraneous factors. In our example, knowing that at most stages of primary schooling girls are better at linguistic activities than boys, we would not want a gender imbalance, because the group with more girls would be likely to perform better for that reason alone, and not because of any intrinsic difference in the effects of the teaching methods.

The second role for random allocation is a rather more complicated one, which we do not treat in detail here but which was, in fact, the original reason why natural scientists used it. It proceeds as follows, by asking: if we actually find a difference in the spelling ability between the two groups at the end of the experiment, is it likely that this difference occurred by chance? And by 'chance' here we mean the engineered chance of the random allocation mechanism. Now, strictly speaking, that meaning of chance is quite different from the usual meaning of chance in social statistics, or indeed social science or social life more generally, which is something to do with what we might call unmeasured hetero-geneity, the random accidents of everyday life. The researcher is deliberately intervening here to introduce uncertainty in order to have control of it. We do not go further into that here, but we set it out in some detail in the Appendix to this chapter. The reason we do not go into it is that, as a justification of randomisation, that argument does not figure very much in the social science discussion of experiments. In the social sciences, it is the first of the two arguments that predominates, the argu-ment that, on average, the two groups will look the same.

The purpose of this random allocation – however interpreted – is to achieve something that is often called 'internal validity'. By internal validity we mean we want to ensure that any conclusions we draw are solidly based. In this particular example, we want to be able to infer that any observed difference in spelling ability is actually caused by the differ-ence in teaching methods. By randomly allocating, we are also able to distinguish between random noise – variation we are not interested in – and real effects of the treatments. The random noise will be less if the people on whom we do the experiment are roughly similar to each other (for example, are all children of the same age). When the noise is less, our conclusions are more reliable: the experiment will have greater power to detect a real difference that may be due to different effects of the treat-ments. The other type of validity – 'external validity' – is discussed in Chapter 3: it is about the capacity of the research to allow valid generali-sation to a wider population and to other times and places.

Our first example of an experiment has been very simple, but it is paradigmatic for all experiments. Here is another example. The way in which it was discovered that a small amount of aspirin taken regularly is quite a good way of preventing heart attacks was through the results of several large experiments in the United States, the UK, Germany and Austria (Canner 1987). A large number of cooperating family doctors randomly gave potential heart attack patients aspirin or a placebo (i.e. a drug that tastes, looks and smells like aspirin but is in fact medically inert). At the end of this experiment, it was discovered that the group who had been given the aspirin had significantly lower incidence of heart attacks than the group that had been given the placebo.

This example illustrates something that is usually regarded as very important in medical experiments but is almost never available in the social sciences. The experiment was 'double-blind'. Neither the patients nor the doctors knew which drug was being given to which patient. The argument for this is to prevent a psychological effect distorting the possible biochemical effect of the drug. The purpose of the study was to look at the effect of the drug, not to look at the effects of knowing that you are on a new drug, or even the effect of your GP's knowing that you are on a new drug (because that knowledge might induce the GP to have certain expectations and so might colour their diagnosis). In medical science, this practice is very common. It is obviously not necessary, on the whole, in science. It does not really matter that pigs know, for example, which particular foodstuffs they are getting. On the other hand, in social science, it is often impossible to ensure that an experiment is double-blind, or even single-blind (i.e. where the subject is unaware of the treatment but the person administering it does know). To see the main reason why, consider an example where a single-blind trial was used.

This study looked at possible racist bias in the shortlisting of candidates for senior posts in hospitals in England (Esmail and Everington 1993). Two researchers submitted a large number of fictitious applications for these posts; on a randomly chosen half of the applications they put Asian names and on the other half they put Anglo-Saxon names. They found that twice as many of the people with Anglo-Saxon names were shortlisted as people with Asian names, even though they had ensured that the two groups had similar qualifications and similar experience, age and so on. In this experiment, the treatment was 'ethnic group' and the thing to which the treatment was being applied was the shortlisting process. Of course, in order to be able to do this experiment, it was necessary not to tell the people to whom this was being applied – the shortlisting committees – that they were actually the subject of an experiment: they were blind to the treatment. Indeed, the researchers were arrested by the police and charged with making fraudulent applications (although they were never tried). The *British Medical Journal*, in which the results were published, pointed out in an editorial the unusual but perhaps necessary nature of this deception as follows:

> we must always question the use of deception in research but in this case the public and professional importance of the question being asked seems to justify the small element of deception.
>
> (BMJ 1993: 668)

However, the very extremity of the situation does illustrate that, in general, it would not be ethically acceptable to do that kind of thing.

Moreover, simply knowing that you are part of an experiment can have an effect on your activity. This is often called the Hawthorne effect, after a study of workers' efficiency at a factory in Hawthorne in the United States (Cook and Campbell 1979: 60; Young 1965: 101ff; Ball 1988: 491–2). The study involved managers altering various aspects of the workplace environment – the lighting, for example – in order to see how productivity could be improved. They appeared to discover that productivity was affected by some of these environmental factors that the managers could control. But then it turned out that a better explanation of these changes in productivity could be that the workers who were not in the control group – the workers who were getting all the attention from the managers, the researchers, and so on – were more productive because their morale had risen as a consequence of getting any attention at all.

There has now emerged an intricate debate as to which of these two interpretations is the most appropriate one – a genuine effect of the treatment, or an effect of being the centre of attention. In some social experiments, this does not matter. For example, Main and Park (1998) describe an experiment in which participants took on certain roles in a law court in order to discover the fairest procedures for inducing the parties to settle cases out of court. The very formalised character of real legal proceedings meant that the artificiality of an experiment was not an impediment to achieving useful results. But, in more natural social situations, the crucial point is that you would not want the results to depend more on the psychology of being studied than on the ostensible topic of that study.

A further general example illustrates the important role for experiments in evaluating policies. The USA's Spouse Assault Replication Program, discussed at length by Boruch (1997: 11–18, 170), was a large set of experiments sponsored by the National Institute of Justice, and eventually including twenty police departments. The main element involved assigning two types of police response to reported incidents of domestic violence – arrest or mediation. These were assigned at random, thus ensuring that the cases which received each treatment were broadly similar in all relevant respects. The analysis concentrated on recidivism, measured both by any further reports to the police of violence after that initial encounter, and evidence from survey interviews to see if the female partner had been assaulted again. We discuss policy research more fully in Chapter 9.

Before we finish this section of examples, it should be noted that the structure of experiments can be much more complicated than the relatively simple illustrations we have given, but the principles do not differ. For example, instead of having just two teaching methods there might be several, or there might be teaching methods combined with some variation in the timetabling (morning or afternoon, say). It also could be the case that, instead of being interested only in whether somebody did or did not get a treatment, you might be interested in the amount of the treatment. That would be more common in medicine, but there would be cases in social science where that might be appropriate as well – for example, the amount of exposure to teaching of a certain subject.

General principles and problems

As we said at the outset of this chapter, the crucial thing about an experiment is intervention. The purpose of random allocation is to ensure control. By control is meant that the group to which you did not apply the treatment is the same as the group that did get the treatment in all relevant characteristics apart from the fact of not receiving the treatment. If that is the case, then we can make valid comparisons between the groups – valid in the sense that any differences which emerge can be attributed to the difference in treatment.

There are four drawbacks of this for investigating human beings.

The first and the most glaring is that intervention might frequently not be ethically acceptable. For example, in the mid-1980s a large study was undertaken in Edinburgh on the effect of exposure to lead on children's development (Fulton *et al.* 1987). It would clearly have been wholly unacceptable to expose children deliberately to lead: even to mention that seems bizarre (as would be the case with almost any pressing social issue such as child abuse, drug taking or unemployment). So what the researchers had to rely on was the naturally occurring variation in exposure to lead that appears in the population of any large city such as Edinburgh. This unacceptability of intervention is found in many circumstances in which we are investigating one specific potentially causal factor.

The second disadvantage is to do with the feasibility of random allocation. Many writers on this say that the problem with random allocation is that it is not ethically acceptable (e.g. Cook and Campbell 1979). More often, however, it is intervention that is not ethically acceptable, and the problem with randomisation is that it can be difficult to achieve. For example, if you wanted to look at the association between children's age and their spelling ability, it would not be possible to allocate randomly because age is not the kind of thing that you randomly allocate; the same would be true of gender or ethnicity. In fact, in most cases where we think about a particular cause of social problems, it would not be possible to allocate that cause randomly. So this is a pragmatic problem, not an ethical one.

Indeed, there are some circumstances in which people would argue that random allocation is the only ethically acceptable thing to do. For example, in studies in the late 1980s into drugs for treating AIDS, because the drugs tended to be in very short supply so that there were insufficient quantities to give to every patient with AIDS, it could be argued that the only morally justifiable thing to do was to give everybody an equal chance of receiving the drugs that were available. So you randomly allocate people to that drug. If you find this puzzling as a moral argument, then ask: given that not enough was known at the time to select on a rational basis patients who would be most likely to benefit, can you think of any other way of allocating the drug that would be more ethically acceptable?

The third point is also pragmatic, and concerns the question of what kind of research you have to be doing in order to be able to do an experiment at all. It is no accident that most experiments in social science are done with captive populations – in prisons, schools, university departments, the army, factories, or in connection with government policies. To do an experiment you have to have some authority over a group being studied, and the power to intervene. That is not to deny that individuals can be offered the chance to opt out, but opting out is more difficult than opting in, especially if the researchers come with the authority of the people in charge of the institution. For example, in research on schools, it may be that the researcher can do something to respect the autonomy of pupils by consulting them and their parents (as would in fact be required by any decent code of ethics). But, nevertheless, we would not be able to get access to the pupils in the first place if we had not first of all gained access to the school hierarchy – the head teacher, the director of education, and so on. This moral dilemma has the pragmatic consequence that it is much more difficult to do experiments with populations where there is no hierarchy of control. If you are doing a community study, for example, there is nobody you can turn to for permission and so no authority you can invoke to induce people to take part. Thus only certain kinds of population can be studied readily by experiment.

The fourth point is an epistemological one. It has to do with what we actually mean by many of the words we have been using in this chapter so far – notably effect, cause and intervention. It may be possible to imagine the natural world as passive, something in which researchers can readily intervene (although the ethical acceptability of this is increasingly in doubt). But that is clearly not the case with human beings. They are not passive subjects but actors. Consider the example of the spelling experiment again: it could well be that the improvement in spelling performance was due to the teacher's enthusiasm for the new method. That could be a version of the Hawthorne effect. But even more subtly than that, the people involved in the experiment can themselves become experimenters. If people know they are in the experiment they can compare how their class is doing with the neighbouring class which is not getting the same method of teaching. That might tend to distort or reinforce the effects of the methods. And even more of a problem would be if the meaning of the teaching method depended on the specific child, so that there is not a common thing called the treatment which is being applied to all the children in the class, in the way that aspirin might be given in a common way to everybody in a medical trial. For example, in exercising normal professional judgement, the teacher might adapt the method to suit the aptitude and motivation of the child, perhaps combining it with elements of other methods that have worked for that child in the past. To do otherwise, it could be argued, would be unprofessional, because it would be to deny that child the opportunities that ought to be available. So the teaching method, the treatment, might actually be something which is negotiated between teacher and child. There would thus be thirty different treatments, one for each of the thirty different children.

One example where this dilemma was unavoidable was in a large-scale experiment on the effects of reducing class size in early primary school conducted in Tennessee in the mid-1980s (Blatchford and Mortimore 1994; Finn and Achilles 1990; Goldstein and Blatchford 1998). Children were allocated at random to small and large classes, as were teachers, and the educational progress was monitored. The problem was that the treatment could hardly be more evident to the participants: every day of the week, children and teachers would be aware that they were in a small or a large class, and would also be aware of the progress that was being made in classes in the same school that were of a different size. This was all the more likely to be a problem because the teachers who took part were volunteers who were likely already to be enthusiasts for the idea that small classes encourage more progress. As Tomlinson (1990: 20) notes:

> the assignment procedure [of teachers to classes] created a surefire situation for engendering disillusionment and disappointment in the [large] class teachers [and] elation and enthusiasm in the small class teachers.

The teachers of the large classes could then regard the whole experiment as a waste of their and their pupils' time.

Quasi-experiments

Despite these problems, researchers have evolved various pragmatic compromises to try to retain some of the advantages of experiments. These designs have been called 'quasi-experiments' (Cook and Campbell 1979). Essentially, the aim has been to find ways of using non-comparable groups, groups whose composition is not strictly controlled. Several types of quasi-experiment can be illustrated by considering various modifications to the example of spelling method with which we started. To get an initial flavour of what a quasi-experiment is, consider what would be possible in the way of inference if, instead of dividing the class in two, we gave the new method to one class and the old method to another class in a different school. This could have the advantage that it did not require new teachers to be employed, did not entail breaking up an intact social group, and reduced the extent to which the two groups might compare themselves with each other. But it also creates problems for deciding whether the spelling method has been effective. It would be very difficult to separate the effects of the different methods from the effects of other differences between the classes. So, as Cook and Campbell (1979) put it, the researcher has to explain specific threats to valid causal inference – specific ways in which the two classes were different. For example, they would have different teachers, maybe a slightly different distribution of ages, or maybe a different gender mix. There would also be the differences that flow from having been in different and fairly stable social groups for some time. Even if the two classes had started out identical when they entered primary school, they would have had different histories in the meantime that might have influenced the children in different ways. The best way of making explicit and taking account of threats to internal validity is to use multivariate statistical methods of analysis.

We shall now look at five main types of quasi-experiment. In none of these is there random allocation by the researchers.

The most valid of these quasi-experiments is where the treatment group and the control group are both measured before and after the experiment. That is, for each group, there is both a pre-test and a post-test. So there are four measurements: a measurement on each group beforehand and a measurement on each group afterwards. In our example, we would have two classes, and we would take a measure of their baseline spelling ability; in other words, their ability before any intervention has happened. Then we do the intervention and test spelling again at the end.

There are several real-life examples of this design. A famous one in Seattle and Denver in the 1970s was an investigation into 'income maintenance', a way of using taxation instead of benefits to compensate for poverty (Burtless and Greenberg 1982; Keeley *et al.* 1978; Kurtz and Spiegelman 1971). Very large numbers of people were involved. Some people received direct social security payments in a conventional way, and other people had income maintenance payments allocated through the tax system. The experimenters studied whether there would be an effect on various things – for example, health, welfare, education, capacity to gain employment. All of these were measured before and after so as to quantify specific threats to the validity of comparisons. But there was no randomisation.

Sometimes, measuring everything beforehand is not easy; indeed, you might not know until afterwards what it was you should have measured, because only once the study has been undertaken do you know what the interesting variables are. So a slightly less strong version of this design is where the groups are matched at the beginning on certain key characteristics – for example, sex and age. In the spelling example, the two classes would be chosen to have the same number of girls in each class, the same age range, and so on. The crucial point here is that the matching characteristics would be chosen to be factors which the literature on the research topic says are associated with the outcome of interest. Thus we would be drawing on what is already known about the phenomenon being studied to find out more about it. Matching has the further advantage of increasing the precision of the experiment: by reducing the amount of extraneous variation, we can more reliably distinguish between random noise and real effects.

The best type of matching is where it happens naturally, in a 'cohort design'. Schools are a good example: they take a sweep of people from more or less the same community every year. For example, there are reasonable grounds for believing that pupils coming into the school in 1999 were, in most respects, similar to the pupils that came in 1998 or 2000. The natural demographics do the matching for you. The big advantage of this design is that you do not have to create artificial experimental groups: you just study the institutions as they are.

An illustration of this use of schools can be found in an evaluation of the Technical and Vocational Education Initiative (TVEI) in Scotland in the 1980s (Paterson 1993). The schools which took part in the TVEI could be compared with schools which did not, and this comparison was quite valid because baseline measures were available on all these schools from periods before the TVEI was even invented. The reason these measures were available was that the Scottish Young Peoples' Survey had been gathering information on all schools every two years since the mid-1970s. The assumption that is required to make the comparison valid here is that successive cohorts of pupils entering the schools would not differ by large amounts.

The second type of quasi-experiment is where there is just one group but there is a pre-test and a post-test. So there is no control group. The problem is then knowing what would have happened otherwise – what would have happened if the researcher had not intervened. Most attempts to evaluate what governments are doing fall into this second category, because very few governments go to the bother and expense of doing experiments. They announce a policy and then sometime later they announce that the policy has succeeded or, possibly, failed (whichever is politically expedient). As social scientists, even if we want to be sceptical about that announcement, we cannot compare what went on under a different policy. The TVEI evaluation was not of this type: by comparing the change over time in the TVEI schools with the change in the non-TVEI schools, some estimate was available of what would have happened in the absence of the TVEI.

The third example is one where there are no pre-tests, but there are two groups – one which gets the treatment and the other which does not. It may be sometimes that this is not as unreasonable as it might first appear, if you have grounds for believing that the two groups are very similar, but these grounds obviously have to be gathered externally to your experiment. For example, you might infer similarity by showing that the two groups were approximately matched on certain demographic characteristics, as in the examples mentioned earlier.

The fourth example of a quasi-experiment is where there is just one group and you only measure it afterwards. Now, in some senses, this is really wholly invalid because you are not making any comparison at all. But this assessment is perhaps not completely fair. It might be that, on theoretical grounds, you could compare the studied group with what you would expect such a group of people to do in similar circumstances. For example, suppose a schoolteacher decides to try out for herself an interesting new teaching method which she has read about in the educational literature. She might not be able to set up an experiment but she might be able, from her own professional knowledge, to compare what actually happens to the children in front of her with what she would have expected to happen with a class like that on the basis of her long experience. This conclusion would not be reliable and so would not be convincing, on its own, as the basis of a generalisation. But it is probably the way in which many research hypotheses are generated: it could be the inspiration for designing a more formally valid study with some degree of proper control. Such investigations are sometimes called action research, because they involve a professional trying out techniques to improve practice.

The fifth type of quasi-experiment is slightly different. Sometimes natural experiments do occur even in the absence of direct intervention by researchers. One that is very often cited is the case of twins being reared apart, and this has been used for investigating the issue of whether environment or genetic inheritance has a greater effect on intelligence

(Gould 1981: 235–6). The point about this example is that you have two people who are identical in all their genetic respects, but who have been assigned to different socialisation treatments (although that simple description conceals the great controversy which surrounds the interpretation of twin studies).

Another example of a natural experiment occurs in Scotland when pupils leave school. The minimum age at which they may do so is 16, which is normally at the end of their fourth year in secondary school, but because about one third of people have their birthday in the months between September and December they have to stay in school for one extra term. The crucial point for research is that this third of pupils is essentially a random selection from all pupils: in most respects, people born in the last third of the year do not differ systematically from people born earlier in the year. So the third who are forced to stay on can be regarded as having been subjected to an experiment, and this point has been used to analyse many of their attitudes and experiences subsequently (Burnhill 1984). For example, it was used to show that even getting a taste of courses taken after fourth year made people more likely to stay on to age 17 and to gain enough qualifications to enter university (Robertson 1993).

The main conclusion to take from this discussion of quasi-experiments is that, when considering a research design, the issue is not the stark one of whether or not it is valid; the point is one of degree – how valid is it? Randomised experiments can be used in some important areas of social science, as we have seen. For most social scientists they are not available. But for all social research, thinking about why a randomised experiment is not feasible is a useful stimulus to assessing how valid the available research designs are. Above all, experiments do provide a clear way of achieving control and therefore of making highly valid comparisons. So comparing our chosen research design with a hypothetical (or actual) experiment on the same topic might clarify the extent to which we have, in fact, failed to control for all threats to validity and therefore have failed to make wholly valid comparisons.

Appendix

Example of the technical role of randomisation in experiments

We give an artificially simple example in order to be able to illustrate the full technical argument. The argument is similar to that which features in discussions of some non-parametric tests in statistical analysis (McNemar 1969). It is sometimes called randomisation inference.

Consider two ways of teaching spelling, labelled A and B, and imagine that we are testing these with four children. Two children are chosen *at random* to be taught by method A. The other two are taught by method B. We assess the spelling ability of all four children at the start of the experiment, and then, at the end, we are able to measure the gain in spelling ability. It is these gains that we concentrate on in the analysis here.

Suppose that (according to some scale of measurement) the gains in marks between the start and the end of the experiment in a spelling test turn out to be:

Two children taught by method A: 11   15

Two children taught by method B: 17   13

Therefore the average gain for A is   13
and the average gain for B is   15

So the difference between B and A is   2

The question now is: could such a big difference as this have occurred *by chance* if there was genuinely *no* difference between the effects of A and B?

The structure of argument is now as follows:

1   *Suppose there is in reality no difference in the effects of the two methods.* Under this hypothesis, then, the difference between the averages in the pairs of children is determined wholly by the randomisation mechanism, because the spelling gain of any particular child would have been the same regardless of which teaching method was used.
2   Calculate on what proportion of all possible allocations of teaching method to pairs of children the average difference would be at least as big as that observed.
3   If this proportion is large, then we conclude that the observed difference could well have occurred by chance.
4   If the proportion is not large, then we conclude that the observed difference was unlikely to have occurred by chance.

To do the calculations required in step 2, we have to calculate what the difference would be under all possible random divisions of the four children into two pairs. Remember that this is still under the hypothesis that there is in reality no difference in the effect of the teaching methods. The display in Table 2.1 shows all possible divisions into pairs, along with what the spelling gains would have been, and the comparison between

Table 2.1 Outcomes of random assignment, under hypothesis of no difference between treatments A and B

A		B		Difference of means (B – A)
11	15	17	13	2
11	15	13	17	2
11	17	15	13	0
11	17	13	15	0
11	13	15	17	4
11	13	17	15	4
15	11	17	13	2
15	11	13	17	2
15	17	11	13	−4
15	17	13	11	−4
15	13	11	17	0
15	13	17	11	0
13	11	17	15	4
13	11	15	17	4
13	17	11	15	−2
13	17	15	11	−2
13	15	11	17	0
13	15	17	11	0
17	11	15	13	0
17	11	13	15	0
17	15	11	13	−4
17	15	13	11	−4
17	13	11	15	−2
17	13	15	11	−2

the average gains in the two methods. In the display, each child is identified by the value of its spelling gain (which is, under the hypothesis, not affected by teaching method).

Still with a view to doing the calculation required for step 2, we note that the numbers of occurrences of each difference are:

−4	4 times
−2	4 times
0	8 times
2	4 times
4	4 times

So a difference as big as the observed one (i.e. 2) occurs on eight occasions (four times exactly, i.e. 2, and four times as 4). This is one-third of the time – the answer to step 2.

In other words, if there were in reality no difference in the effects of the two teaching methods, a difference in average spelling gain as big as the one we did get could occur by chance on one-third of occasions.

For the remaining steps in the argument, it is a matter of judgement whether this proportion of one-third is large. Conventionally, large is defined as anything bigger than one in twenty (5 per cent). So this is large, and so we are at the conclusion in step 3. In other words, the observed difference could well have occurred by chance even if there were in reality no difference in the effects of the two teaching methods. Hence we conclude that we have no convincing evidence that the two methods do differ.

3   Representativeness

How are we able to infer that an observed relationship can be generalised? In the previous chapter, we saw that the point of experiments was to set up conditions under which we could infer that an observed relationship was meaningful – that one thing caused another, or at least was an explanation of it. And although the question of generalisation is in practice inescapable with experiments, it is secondary to internal validity, because unless you are sure that what you have observed actually happened and actually meant something, there is nothing to generalise about at all. Sometimes generalisability is called 'external validity'. The aim is to allow valid comparisons between the sample and the population from which it came by controlling any differences between the sample and that population.

There are three sections in this chapter. The first is about representative samples, which is the ideal type of representativeness – something to which, in some ways, we are always trying to approximate when we select a sample. The second section is briefer: it is about the unavoidable departures from that ideal type, even when we are attempting to select a representative sample of a statistical sort. And then in the last section we ask more broadly what do we want representativeness for.

Representative samples

In understanding the uses to which representative samples can be put, it is relevant to note that their origins early in the twentieth century are closely connected with reforming social science – that strand in European social science that became, in one tradition, social democracy, and, in another, communism. In fact, some of the very notable early users of representative samples were of this sort: Rowntree and Booth in late nineteenth-century England, and Lenin, who started his professional life as a statistician in the then imperial Russian Ministry of Agriculture.

ı these people believed that what they were doing was collecting ınation in order to change the world, and the world that they wanted change was this relatively new concept of a society – a collection of ndividuals who, in some senses, were very similar to each other (Hacking 1975). The revolution in thinking that took place, roughly between the end of the eighteenth century and the middle of the nineteenth century, was the advent of the idea that in order to find out characteristics of that whole population, it was not necessary to measure the whole population. It was sufficient to look at a sample and, in fact, at a relatively small sample. The ideas that evolved from then, and that have been developed in the twentieth century, produced two different ways of selecting that sample so that it could provide us with adequate descriptions of the population as a whole.

Random sampling

The first way is often described as 'random sampling'. The arguments for a random sample are similar to the arguments in the last chapter for 'random allocation' in experiments. To see this, consider a simplified example. Suppose that we are looking for a sample of size 5,000 to investigate voting behaviour in Britain. The argument for random selection goes like this. If we select a sample at random from a list of the people in Britain – the sampling frame, for example the Electoral Register – then on average it will be representative of the population in all respects. For example, this means that, in Britain, there will be roughly 2,600 women and 2,400 men, because 52 per cent of the British population are women. What is more, if we did this sampling over and over again, although each sample would produce a different female proportion, these would cluster around the true population value of 52 per cent, and on average the proportion in the sample who were female would be exactly the same as this population proportion. Although no one person or organisation ever does do it over and over again, the point from the last chapter comes in – that we have to *imagine* a whole lot of other similarly inclined rational investigators doing this sampling.

What we have done here is deliberately introduce a degree of randomness. We have built this in because, in return for it, we get two things. One is that we know that the sample is representative, and that characteristics calculated from the sample will be roughly the same as the analogous characteristics for the population. For example, in a voting behaviour study, the proportion in the sample intending to vote for a particular political party will be the same as the proportion in the population. Or rather, the proportions will be the same within certain bounds.

And this is the second advantage that we obtain: the error bounds can be measured. We can say that there is a high likelihood that the true value in the population lies within some distance of the measured value in the sample. This book is not about the analysis of data, and so we do not go into the technical matter of the calculation of these error bounds. The point is that a particular design will allow the bounds to be calculated. We have controlled the degree of unrepresentativeness in order to make comparisons with the population that are valid within certain measurable limits. The extent of these limits is the reliability of the design: tighter limits mean more reliable conclusions. This is analogous to the points about reliability in experiments which we made in Chapter 2.

The other important starting point for this very simple example of a random sample is rather surprising, and is contrary to popular belief. The measurable error is almost unrelated to the fraction of the total population which the sample represents; it relates mainly to the absolute size of the sample. So, for example, if you have a sample of size 2,000, then the degree of error is the same, whether it came from a population of 5 million or from a population of 250 million. (However, if the sampling fraction – the proportion of the population in the sample – is greater than about 10 per cent, then the relative size of the sample does begin to have an effect.)

The main refinement of simple random sampling is directed at the inadequacy of relying on the sample's being representative on average over repeated samples. It might be epistemologically adequate to say that, on average, 2,600 of the 5,000 will be women. It might also be an acceptable reassurance to infer from this that, in any one particular sample, this will be approximately true. But these approximate arguments are not always enough. Suppose, for example, that we want to have an adequate basis for studying ethnic minority groups in Scotland, which there make up only about 1 per cent of the adult population. Then, out of a sample of 5,000 only about fifty, on average, would come from these groups, and this would fluctuate quite a lot from sample to sample. In fact, in about one sample in twenty, the number in the minority ethnic groups would be less than thirty-five or more than sixty-five. Numbers as small as thirty-five would be an inadequate basis for making a study of such groups.

So, in response to the problem that any particular random sample may by chance not be sufficiently representative of some characteristic in which we are interested, the procedure of stratification has been invented. This is the most important idea in sampling after randomness itself. Again, the idea is quite simple. Instead of relying on chance, we deliberately force the sample to be representative with respect to a small number of key characteristics. In our first example, we would deliberately choose

2,600 women and 2,400 men, thus ensuring that the sample would be representative with respect to sex; this would be described as having been stratified by sex. Which women you take and which men you take is then decided randomly. So you randomly select 2,600 people from the list of all women, and 2,400 from the list of all men. The sample is guaranteed to be representative with respect to sex, and, on average, it will be representative with respect to all other characteristics because it has been randomly sampled within each of the two categories of sex.

That example is a very simple form of stratification. You could have much more complicated forms. Still with our sample of 5,000 British voters, suppose you wanted it to be representative with respect to age, geographical area and sex. These would be three stratifying factors. Suppose too there were five age groups, ten geographical areas and two sexes. This gives you 100 strata altogether, because each combination of age group, geographical area and sex gives you a particular sub-group of the population with respect to which you want the sample to be representative. For example, you want to be sure that the proportion in the sample who are female from the North of England and are aged 30–44 is the same as the proportion in the population of Britain who come from that region and who are that sex and who are that age. The sample would now be guaranteed to be representative with respect to all three of the stratifying factors. Moreover, if the sample members were selected at random within each of the 100 strata, then the sample would be representative, on average, with respect to everything else. So this sample design has combined a degree of determinacy (the strata) with a degree of indeterminacy so as to cover everything else that has not been built in. An incidental advantage of stratification is that the reliability is increased: because we have explicitly controlled for some sources of variation (here, age, area and sex) the remaining random variation is smaller and so our conclusions are more firmly based.

The choice of strata can be difficult, and there are no mathematical rules to allow you to do it. It involves judgement, a point to which we return in the last section of this chapter. The general point, however, is to stratify with respect to factors that you think are related to the main object of study. For example, if you were studying attitudes to pension rights, then age would be an important stratifying factor, and so also would sex be in those societies where there are sex differences in pension rights. But something like eye colour or height would not be relevant. In practice, usually the same list of things are judged to be relevant to most social investigations: sex, age, social class, region, and some other demographic factor such as health status or religion. The popularity of these might be partly because they are fairly easy to measure, or at least are thought to be so. It is also true that many sociological and other social science theories do involve these variables.

One obstacle to stratifying is that the list – the sampling frame – from which we choose our sample must contain, for each member of the population, information on the stratifying factors – here, age, sex, social class and geographical area. Such lists are rare.

Another problem in choosing strata is that you very quickly run out of enough people in your sample to fit into all the strata. In our example where there were only three stratifying factors, we ended up with as many as 100 strata. If we had introduced another classification, for example social class with five categories, we would have 500 strata, which would give us approximately ten people in each. With such small numbers, any particular sample is almost bound to be unrepresentative with respect to those characteristics that have not been listed among the stratifying factors (and there are likely to be many, because many factors will not be listed on the sampling frame). For example, among the ten chosen men aged 30–44 in the professional social class in a particular area, we might by chance find that we had only university graduates, even though not all such men in the population are graduates. Thus the more strata we have, the less possible it is to rely on the argument that randomness will create strata which are approximately representative with respect to all the unmeasured characteristics.

In practice, stratification is very often combined with clustering. If a sample were selected simply at random from the whole population, then the sample members would be scattered very widely. That can be awkward if the survey is to be conducted by interviewing (as discussed further in Chapters 5 and 6). So the sample could be selected in two stages. Consider our example again, and suppose we are using the Electoral Register as the sampling frame. In the first stage, a stratified random sample of constituencies would be taken; in the second, we would select a random sample of people within each of these selected constituencies. Thus the individuals in the final selected sample would be clustered within constituencies, and so would be reasonably accessible to a team of interviewers. Moreover, data for stratifying the constituencies would be more readily available than data for stratifying the selection of individuals. There are consequences for the analysis from clustering, mainly because the random error is increased, but the gain in accessibility compensates for any such complications.

Quota sampling

The other method of selecting a sample is called 'quota sampling'. This is far more common than random sampling because it is the standard method in the market research industry (which includes opinion polls). The reason it is so widely used is that it is more feasible in more situations than random sampling. In particular, it overcomes the need for a sampling frame.

To see how quota sampling works, consider again the same sample as was discussed above. The total sample size is 5,000, and we want the sample to be representative with respect to five age groups, ten geographical areas and two sexes. A quota sample could be organised as follows. In each of the ten geographical areas, a sample would be aimed at which ensured that the area made up the same proportion of the sample as it did of the population. For example, this would mean that about 9 per cent of the 5,000, or 450, ought to come from Scotland. Accordingly, we would set out to sample 450 people in Scotland. About ten interviewers would be recruited to deal with this, each having to interview forty-five people. The interviewers are crucial to the next step in selecting the sample. Their instructions are that they have to find forty-five people who are exactly representative with respect to the other two specified characteristics, age and sex. For example, out of the Scottish population approximately 11 per cent are men aged 30–44, and approximately 11 per cent are women of this age. So the interviewers would have to find about five men of this age, and about five women (since 11 per cent of forty-five is five): these are the interviewer's 'quota' within these categories. The same kind of rules would be used for each age group, and also for the interviewers in each of the other geographical areas.

The result of this process is that the sample is guaranteed to be representative with respect to geographical area, sex and age group. The word 'quota' in quota sampling corresponds to the word 'strata' in random sampling, and factors such as age and sex are sometimes called 'quota controls'. But this is where the difference from random sampling comes in. The interviewer in quota sampling is free to choose any five men and any five women within the age bands. The sample is guaranteed to be representative with respect to the characteristics specific in the quota controls, just as it was with respect to the strata in the stratified random sample. But, unlike random sampling, the sample might be quite unrepresentative with respect to other characteristics. It is only guaranteed to be representative – even on average – if we can translate the phrase 'select *any* five men' as a *random* five men, and '*any* five women' as a *random* five women.

Only if the interviewer is operating in a random way will the rules of random sampling operate.

Much of the training that is given to interviewers in quota sampling is directed towards trying to get them to select in a random way. The first step to improving the quality is to insist that interviews take place in the relative privacy and tranquility of people's homes – not in the street. Indeed, street interviewing – although common in some market research – is not advisable for any research that aspires to be rigorous. Having established this, the next step is to ensure that the selection of homes is, in effect, random. For example, suppose an interviewer knocks on a door knowing that they still have to find one woman aged 30–44. If the household turns out not to contain such a person, then an interview cannot take place. So the interviewer has to decide which door to knock on next. The rules that the interviewer gets for this try to ensure randomness: for example, after leaving this house, the interviewer would have to turn left or right according to some random instruction, and would then walk past a randomly specified number of doors before trying again. These random rules would have been set by the researchers in charge of the survey, and would be listed on a series of cards for the interviewer; a different card would be used each time the interviewer had to move to a new address.

Because of these fairly elaborate rules which interviewers are given for operating quota samples, most people analysing them treat them as if they were random samples. In particular, whenever you read reports of opinion polls in newspapers, this is what they are doing. When the more ostensibly sophisticated newspapers quote 'error bounds' as they now tend to do, they are operating as if the sample had been a random sample. Whether or not that is a valid assumption, one thing which it certainly does not take into account is the implicit clustering which quota sampling induces. Just as with clustered random sampling, the group of people interviewed by one particular interviewer will tend to live quite close together. So the true random error will be greater than for a simple, unclustered random sample.

What goes wrong in practice with representativeness

Before we discuss some of the wider questions of representativeness, we look at two important ways in which these attempts at representative sampling always fall down in practice. These are not just things that happen when you are unlucky; they are certain to happen. The first is to do with the coverage of the sampling frame. The sampling frame is a list of the people that are available to be selected. But that list is almost never, in fact, compiled for the purposes of academic research. It is usually produced for some administrative purpose. In Britain, the most common sampling frame was until recently the Electoral Register, the list of people entitled to vote. This list is not produced for the purposes of selecting samples from it, and is not an absolutely reliable list of adults. It does not include recent arrivals from abroad, and it includes some people twice – for example, those who have recently moved house.

There are all sorts of other lists which sometimes have to be used but which cause their own problems. For example, telephone subscribers are, on the whole, more socio-economically advantaged than people who do not have telephones. So if you are interviewing by telephone, then you have a list of people that is not the population you might want to study but just a list of people who have a telephone. The Postcode Address File is a list of all the dwellings in the UK, and is a useful sampling frame, much better than the telephone directory, and is becoming more popular for sampling than the Electoral Register. But, if it is to be used to yield a sample of individuals rather than buildings, then it has to be combined with some scheme for sampling people within dwellings. This adds an extra complication, and therefore more expense.

Very generally, because most of these lists emanate from some type of bureaucracy, they are biased towards including only people who are part of society, who want to be in touch with society's official agencies. There might well be groups in society who simply refuse to take part. The most obvious example in Britain was the effects that the poll tax of 1989–92 had on the Electoral Register. Almost certainly it depressed voter registration in some places because people did not want to be registered for the tax. The Postcode Address File, although covering more of the population than the Electoral Register, does exclude some groups, for example residents on travellers' sites.

So this is the first problem, that the sampling frame will not always correspond exactly to the population you might want to study (although sometimes it will be very close). This first problem affects only random sampling, not quota sampling.

The other main departure from the ideal type affects both: refusal, or people not wanting to take part in your sample. This would not matter if the people who did take part were themselves a representative sample. But all the evidence is that the people who take part are not representative of the whole. In fact, several studies in Britain indicate that, when compared to people who do not take part in surveys, people who agree to be interviewed are more likely to be female, middle-class, have a lot of education, to be young, to be living in rural areas, and not to be living in the south of England. Precise details of this list do not matter; the point is that there are important ways in which respondents differ from people who refuse.

In addition, quota sampling is found to be biased in certain other ways, very obviously towards people who are accessible. A person who is hardly ever in their house is very unlikely to be the person who answers the door to the interviewer in search of a quota. There is also a bias resulting from the fact that if we decide not just to stop people in the street because it enables us to use rules leading to greater randomness, we introduce a different kind of bias, towards people living in large households. When interviewers knock on doors, they are both more likely to find someone at home and more likely to find a suitable person to interview if the household is large. (Accessibility is also a problem for random sampling: although the interviewer can be – and nearly always is – instructed to return to houses where the listed sample member was not at home on the first call, there is nevertheless a practical limit to the number of times that repeat visits can be made.) The important point, in general, is that the problem of refusals is an unavoidable problem for all academic research. You cannot compel people to agree to being interviewed. Even the census in countries where it is compulsory by law, which it is in the UK, cannot compel people to cooperate because some people, on grounds of conscience, refuse to take part and choose to pay the fine that results.

The purpose of representativeness

This last section raises some wider questions about the role of representativeness. As with experiments, we have to ask whether the technology of random or quota sampling has become an end in its own right, and how much it is actually dealing with real epistemological issues that we want to address. The purpose of randomness here, unlike in experiments, is for comparability with the population, and the same purpose is partly fulfilled by the concept of stratification or quotas. In other words, the purpose is to have a research design that will enable us to generalise from the sample to the population. But what do we mean here by generalisability? We mean precisely this and only this: if the sample has been chosen in one of the ways that we have looked at, then we can infer that a description of the sample is also a description of the population, with the relatively minor caveat that there will be some measurable uncertainty.

Now, sometimes, as was indicated in Chapter 1, description may be all that we want. This would be the case with what are often called accounting statistics, the kind of thing which government statisticians do virtually all the time. It would then be important to produce an accurate picture of what society is like, and drawing inferences about that picture would not be the statistician's job. This is also what commercial auditors do: they might have to describe the balance sheet of a company, and sometimes they will do that by sampling records (for example, invoices). But in academic research – as we also argued in Chapter 1 – it is very rare indeed that pure description is all that we want. Nearly always we want to explain as well.

So we are back to the same kind of question as we asked for experiments. The question is not: is this sample representative of the population? It is the more subtle question: is what we have observed representative of the type of situation we claim to be studying? Making sense of that phrase 'type of situation' is a matter of judgement, of intuition, of your prior theoretical framework, and it concerns these much more than it does the technology of random or quota sampling. So the question about representativeness is a much broader and deeper question.

Consider an example (for further details of which, see Campbell 1987; Christy 1987; Lovenduski and Norris 1993). Suppose we are studying the question of 'the effect of gender on voting behaviour in elections', and suppose that amongst a group of women and men whom we observe, the women are found to be more likely to vote Conservative. Now, to go from that description to some theoretically interesting statement – in other words, to infer that there is a 'gender' effect – we have to ask: can it be generalised to other men and other women? Indeed, it is difficult to make sense of a term like 'gender' unless we can generalise in that sort of way. But, of course, obviously we are not saying that all women vote Conservative or that all men do not vote Conservative. We are claiming that women tend to be more likely to vote Conservative than men. We would test that hypothesis not merely by taking a particular sample, but by looking at lots of types of women and men to ensure that as many different types of circumstance had been taken into account. If we found that more women than men vote Conservative in all of these types, or perhaps in most of these types, then we might conclude that there was indeed a gender effect on voting Conservative. So we are inferring, from a greater proportion of women voting Conservative in lots of different circumstances, to a greater tendency for women to vote Conservative.

There are two problems with this kind of inference as a means to generalisation. The first is somewhat similar to a problem in the last chapter about experiments. For example, consider another characteristic of the people under study – social class. What if social class operates differently for men and women? You would find in most studies that, despite our hypothesis, working-class women would be less likely to vote Conservative than middle-class men. So we control for class: we stratify by class or we put in a quota control for class, and we look at the voting behaviour between men and women in different social classes. But although that seems a natural move, it is not immediately obvious why we are entitled to give epistemological primacy to class. Why are we saying that the gender effect exists only if it is manifested among people of similar class? What is it that allows us to control for class before asking a question about gender? What if the class identity of, say, a man is intimately related to his masculinity? Then 'controlling' for class is actually removing part of the gender effect we want to study.

So the question then is: what do we mean by 'type of situation' in our definition of generalisable? We said that the gender difference would be inferred only if it was manifested in many types of situation – i.e. in lots of examples. Why do we say that the workings of gender within each social class is an *example* of the effect of gender? Might it not be that the effect of gender within each social class is unique, and therefore is not an example of anything more general? There is no straightforward answer (we return to this point in our discussion of case studies in Chapter 4).

The second problem concerns social and personal change. What happens, in fact, if our gender difference disappears? This is what has been happening in Britain since the late 1980s. None of the technology for selecting random samples, whether quota or random, would have coped with that change. If you had selected a sample in 1983, you would have found more women voting Conservative than men. The point is that the sample would have been representative only of that point in time, and we would have had to exercise our judgement to decide whether that particular moment was sufficient for making a generalisation.

So, again, what do we mean by generalising? When we said that there was a gender effect in 1983, were we claiming that this was a gender effect for all time, that it was something intrinsic to femaleness and maleness, or were we making a very time-bound statement, a statement about femaleness and maleness only at that moment in time? We discuss time in much more detail in Chapter 7, because time is always a major problem for doing research that we think can be generalised.

A version of this problem concerns time within individuals – not just the age of individuals but the time at which we observe them. When we say somebody is a woman or a man we are positing some characteristic that is somehow constant about them, but the consequences of that characteristic might not be constant, which might limit the scope for generalisation. Some electoral studies have found that the apparent gender effect on voting disappears when age is controlled for: women appear to be more likely to vote Conservative than men, but this can be explained away by the fact that women as a whole tend to live longer, with the result that women as a group contain more older people (who tend to be somewhat Conservative-inclined) than men as a group. But this control for age raises the same kind of question as the control for class: what allows us to give primacy to age, so that a gender effect can be said to exist only if it is manifest at all (or most) particular ages? (A very thorough discussion of age as a variable in social research is provided by Rutter (1989).)

So representativeness is actually a difficult concept. It is difficult to achieve, and requires a great deal of skill, and this is true whether or not we are using statistically representative samples. You have to use judgement to decide whether that which you are studying is typical of all other relevant situations that you might want to study – whether you really have controlled for all or most of the relevant differences between your sample and the population to which you want to generalise. Ultimately, the purpose of representativeness is as a form of persuasion. It is a means by which you try to convince other people that what you have studied is typical of what they might want to have studied, or typical of what they understand by the terms that you are using, for example gender. You want to persuade them that you have controlled for potential ways in which the sample might be untypical. Persuading people is an important part of research: you have to be able to have your results accepted by other people before they can be properly discussed. In appropriate circumstances, the way to persuade people of your study's representativeness is by the type of sampling we discussed in the first section of the chapter. But even there, the technical competence of the sampling is not enough in itself to prove that the study is representative. There are forms of judgement that have to be exercised as well – for example, the choice of the time at which you do your sampling, or the choice of strata or quota controls. Where your research does not use sampling of this type, you still have to consider representativeness, and to find other ways of persuading people that what you have done is typical of some wider context.

4 The choice of locale and group

Decisions about where to carry out a piece of research, and on whom to focus, lie at the very heart of research design. The process of making these decisions depends largely on imagination, ingenuity and a capacity for lateral thinking rather than the straightforward application of scientific principle. We touched obliquely on this uncomfortable truth in the previous chapter. The issue with which we ended the chapter might be characterised as the *what* and *why* of representativeness. We have to know clearly what we wish a sample or study to be representative of, and why we want it to be representative in this way. Underlying these questions is the more fundamental one of just what we wish a particular piece of research to address and why we are interested in this.

The choice of locale and group would be more straightforward if deciding to carry out and designing a piece of research followed a neat linear path. It is tempting to think that this is indeed what happens, and this belief is reinforced by the somewhat idealised accounts of empirical work which often appear in the literature. The social scientist, steeped in the literature of a specialised topic, sees that a theory, be it about voting behaviour, patterns of cohabitation and marriage, the underlying causes of unemployment or why revolutions occur when they do, is flawed or needs to be extended. Further reflection suggests an answer to this weakness in, or to this lack of scope of, the theory. The social scientist then sets out to explore whether this is indeed an adequate answer, choosing to investigate particular individuals or groups in particular places as is determined by the revised theory. The choice of locale and group follows smoothly from the problem in hand.

While the process is hardly ever quite as logically linear as that, some-times it is indeed a reasonable approximation to what happens. In a study which depends on a national population survey, especially if the analysis is secondary, carried out on an already existing data set, the locale and group are clearly determined in advance or indeed were determined by someone else. The social scientist is interested in a particular issue, problem or puzzle, and decides that large amounts of data, representative of the population in question, are what is needed. A national survey is designed, or a previous one found which contains the kind of data one wants. Thus an examination of why political events in Scotland took the form they did in 1997, the year of the general election which left the Conservative Party with no seats in Scotland, and of the referendum voting to set up a Scottish Parliament, manifestly required a large-scale national survey of the Scottish electorate (Brown *et al.* 1999).

In a great deal of research, however, especially the kind of small-scale research often carried out by tyro researchers such as graduate students, the business of choosing a group and locale emerges from a much messier process, where the interest springs from a far less clearly refined set of issues, or where the broad characteristics of the group to be studied, if not the locale, are determined by a curiosity about some aspects of their behaviour, beliefs or attitudes. The more exploratory a piece of research, the more likely that the choice of group and place is made in the course of a cyclical process, whereby this aspect of the research and the topics to be addressed are both progressively refined in order to produce the research design over a considerable period of time.

Researchers, especially inexperienced ones, sometimes fall into a trap here. They are interested in carrying out exploratory research on a particular phenomenon and assume that the group and place are self-evident. This is especially tempting in research on a particular occupational group or some policy-related work. If one wishes to study the workings of a drug rehabilitation scheme, midwives on a hospital labour ward, or the process of offering contraceptive advice to young people, the subjects of the research and where they are to be found may seem to be unproblematic. The uncertain issues perhaps appear to be those of access, or method. Perfectly respectable research can be and often is designed and carried out in this way. However, it could often be more exciting and effective if more attention had been paid to the processes which lie at the heart of this book – comparison and control. A research locale may be compared with another, not always self-evident locale; the group being studied may be better chosen in a less obvious way, or compared to a group which is not obvious at first sight. For example, in Chapter 1 we referred to Glaser and Strauss choosing an alternative emergency service as comparator, rather than another emergency ward.

Our point here is then quite simple, but it is fundamental. The task of deciding exactly what the research issues are and arriving at a suitably focused and sharp set of research questions is not independent of the task of deciding where the study will be carried out and which groups or indi-

viduals will be involved. It requires a process of reflection and imagination as well as professional knowledge. It involves paying careful attention
to comparison and control. It cannot be done by rote. It is undeniable
that research design involves an element of creativity which cannot be
straightforwardly codified or taught. This is of course not confined to
social science. In the experimental branches of the physical and biological
sciences, enormous ingenuity may be required to think of and design an
experiment that addresses a problem. There is an excellent discussion of
these issues as they affect natural scientists in Ian Hacking's book
Representing and Intervening (1983). Hacking's analysis repays study by
social scientists too. Similarly, what it is that one should do, which
involves where one should do it and with what groups, may in the social
sciences require a leap of imagination that separates competent from
outstanding researchers.

Many years ago, a very neat, if dubiously ethical, procedure was used by
ethnomethodologists to establish that people will under certain circumstances make sense of what are in fact nonsensical and random
interactions (Garfinkel 1967: 79–94). Students in the USA were told that
a new counselling procedure would allow them to ask any questions they
wished of an unseen counsellor but the questions must allow of a 'yes' or
'no' answer. The answers to the students' questions were randomly 'yes' or
'no' and thus frequently entirely inconsistent one with another. It was
found that, astonishingly, students made sense of the responses and were
able to mould them into an overall pattern. The students were of course
subsequently debriefed and made aware of the deception. We would not
recommend such a procedure, and it is doubtful if it should ever have
been carried out, but its ingenuity is undeniable. Few researchers would
have thought of it.

The best research designs – as we suggested at the beginning – are the
ones which lead others to say 'I wish I'd thought of that' or 'Yes, that's
obviously the way to do it'. What is interesting here is that it is only
'obvious' after someone has thought of it. However, the new researcher
should not despair. Although in the last analysis it is undeniable that
some people are better at making the imaginative leap which produces
the outstanding design, excellent research is done with more standard
approaches, and up to a point researchers can learn to improve their
designs. We shall return to this later in the chapter.

First, however, we shall discuss one particular design, the case study,
where the choice of group and place is integral to the research. We pay
particular attention to case studies here because the choice of a case, and
what is meant by a case, illustrate some general difficulties about choosing
what and whom to study.

What are case studies?

When we speak of a 'case study', it is interesting that we seldom feel any necessity to define just what is involved, and indeed the meaning of the phrase is generally clear from the context. This usage does, however, hide a wide variation in the meaning of the word 'case'. The level of analysis is relevant to, but does not determine, whether we think of something as a 'case'. In a comparative study of a number of nations, each nation would be a case. Yet we would not generally refer to the study of each of the nations as a case study, although this would not be inappropriate. Similarly, in a survey with 200 respondents, we might speak of having 200 cases; tables frequently supply the reader with 'N of cases'. But here we would not think of the data relating to each respondent as a case study. If the respondents all came from a particular organisation, such as a school, a factory or a political party, then the survey might indeed be part of a case study of that school, factory or party. We would think of it being a case study at the level of the organisation.

It does not follow that an individual cannot be the subject of a case study. There is a long history of studies of individuals, or of a relatively small number of individuals of a particular kind (for early examples, see for instance Anderson 1923; Shaw 1930). The study of the life-course is a powerful research design which we discuss further in Chapter 8.

This brief account of the variety of ways in which we use the word indicates that the idea of a case is fundamental to social enquiry. For the purposes of this book it will suffice if the reader bears in mind that case studies can take many forms.

The most common usage of the term 'case study' is immediately relevant to the choice of group and locale with which we are concerned in this chapter. If we choose to study a group of children in a classroom, doctors and nurses in an accident and emergency ward, workers in a particular machine shop or union branch, or people working in an organisation such as the BBC, most social scientists would think of this as a case study, and the use of such a research design requires us to justify the choice of group and locale.

Two incorrect views of case studies

We turn next to two critical views of the case study which are not unusual but which we regard as misplaced. Social scientists of an experimental or especially positivistic turn of mind sometimes ask how one can generalise from a single case. Put in this way, by these critics, the question is absurd. As we pointed out in the previous chapter, exactly the same issue arises in the case of the single experiment. What is remarkable is that the question of how one can generalise from an experiment is seldom asked. This may be a consequence of the classic exemplar of an experiment in people's minds being drawn from the physics or chemistry to which they were exposed in their schooldays. Underlying these experiments is the assumption that the nature of chemical and physical processes is invariant over time and place, if certain conditions are held constant. For a great deal of standard experimentation this assumption appears to be sound, but it does depend on the holding constant of the appropriate conditions. Experiments may, for instance, have to be carried out under conditions where temperature is closely controlled or the apparatus is shielded from electric fields.

When we apply similar ideas to experiments in social science we immediately see that while internal validity may be high, and this is the justification for the experiment, generalisation is not as easy as it appears to be in the physical sciences. A ready belief in the external validity of the experiment, in our ability to generalise, rests on a misunderstanding of what is going on in the model we are adopting. There are two classic problems confronting us: first, that we simply do not understand adequately what the conditions are which we would need to control; and second, that processes involving human beings cannot be assumed to be invariant. We do not intend to address here the question of whether in principle social science might aspire to the precision of the physical and biological sciences. What matters for our purposes is that this is, at this moment in time, certainly not the case.

The second view of the case study which we wish to discard is that there is some kind of ranking of research designs which places experiments above others. This view sees the case study, usually carried out by qualitative methods, as essentially exploratory. It is regarded as an excellent way to obtain a preliminary understanding which will then be developed further by moving to more quantified approaches such as the survey, and eventually the experiment as the appropriate design to establish causality. From the earlier chapters it should be clear that we reject this position. We explained in Chapter 2 why experiments should not be viewed in this way in social science. Furthermore, each research design has to be individually tailored to achieve the aims and objectives of the research, paying due attention to the appropriate comparisons and the issues of control. For instance, sometimes we want to establish how measurements of some concept are distributed in a population, how they are associated with others, whether they can be built into a more formal model, and so on. Generally, the appropriate design will be a survey. If we already know quite a lot about these phenomena we may be able to design our survey straightaway. We may be helped by existing interview schedules used by other people, and items obtained from a survey question bank. When we have results from our survey we may wish to pursue some of the issues more intensively at a level of detailed meaning which the survey does not permit. Further interviews of some kind, semi-structured or even unstructured, or focus groups would be a way of proceeding. Occasionally, if the survey was of a relatively small and accessible population, a period of participant observation might be used. On the other hand, where we know very little about the problem in hand, it may indeed be a good idea to do qualitative work first, possibly a case study or several case studies, so that we can then try and develop our survey schedule on the basis of what we find.

Generalisation from case studies

If we rephrase the inappropriate question about generalisation from a single case to ask *in what sense* a case study is representative, it becomes more meaningful. In a strictly statistical sense, we cannot generalise at all from a case study. If we carry out research on an organisation, be it a voluntary association or a financial institution, it would clearly be unwise to assume that all voluntary associations or all financial institutions, or to be even more extreme all organisations, must exhibit the same characteristics or behave in the same way. However, if the reader is sympathetic to the comment that generalising to all organisations would be more extreme, we can begin to see that there are indeed issues of judgement involved. It does seem *a priori* more likely that all financial institutions will behave similarly in certain ways. And if we narrow the field further to, say, clearing banks, we might feel more confident that our study could be tentatively generalised. A little further reflection suggests that we would probably wish to qualify this further. If we are studying personnel policies, then – subject to the pressures of the labour market and generally agreed 'best policies' – there might be wide variation between the banks. However, hypothetically we might also think that the way this bank goes about determining the way it handles its funds is more likely to be similar to the procedures of other banks.

This suggests that there is more to this question of generalisation than judgement alone. Our judgement is likely to be greatly affected by our conceptual understanding of the way this process of fund-handling works. We might think that the way a bank handles its funds is likely to be affected by the legal and fiscal environment, and thus be happier to think of our bank as representative of British banks. There will be economic and financial theories which are relevant here, and again we may think that these are sufficiently general as to affect all banks. What is involved here is the general argument which we reviewed in the first chapter when we were discussing the ideas of Glaser and Strauss. Case studies may be seen as representative and generalisable insofar as we are trying to generate and develop theories. Generalisation is analytic and not statistical. This can lead us into a position which is in some regards counter-intuitive, and which we also addressed briefly in the first chapter. We have already referred again to Glaser and Strauss's point that rather than replicating a study, we should move on to conceptually similar but apparently contrasting situations. The findings of our case study on the bank may be generalisable to other organisations which for theoretical reasons we think may behave in a similar way. Alternatively, we may look more speculatively at an organisation that is quite different from a bank – for example, an educational institution or a large retail chain – to test how far our findings from the bank can be extended.

So to the extent that a case study illuminates and develops theory, we may treat it as representative. The research represents not so much all voluntary organisations or all financial institutions, but the empirical manifestation of some aspect of social theory.

Evaluation and the case study

Social scientists are frequently involved in evaluating a particular procedure or the way in which something is organised. Evaluation studies is now a very well-developed area which we cannot tackle in any detail (although we return briefly to them in our discussion of policy research in Chapter 9). Readers wishing to carry out this kind of work or learn more about it are referred to the specialist literature. We restrict ourselves here to a few comments about the part played by case studies.

Some kinds of evaluation are carried out on a very large scale. Clinical trials in medicine can involve large numbers of patients, and elaborate experimental designs with several experimental and control groups. Procedures may be put into place to ensure that only the experimenters know which actually are the experimental and control groups, so that clinicians evaluating the outcomes are not influenced by knowing which group is expected to do better than another. The methodology does not have to be that of the experiment. The results of large surveys may be compared to assess the impact of some event or change.

Much smaller-scale evaluations, however, are extremely common: those which assess the state of affairs or changes in small units such as a classroom, a school, an organisation or a hospital ward. In Chapter 2 we referred to one of the most famous examples of this kind of work, the

Hawthorne experiments. This research, as we described, started life as a straightforward experimental study of the impact of illumination on productivity. The experimenters would no doubt, on sound theoretical grounds, have expected that the results would be generalisable to other industrial settings if indeed they were the result of the changes in illumination. When it became clear to the investigators that something rather different seemed to be going on, in time they came to the conclusion that this was not the case and that the results had to be explained by group processes. Theoretical explanations were offered, and these spawned a vast number of other studies and indeed changes in industrial practice. The major consequence of the Hawthorne experiments was the so-called 'human relations movement'. Although the validity of the conclusions drawn has since been called into question, there can be no doubt that the experiment and its successors are a classic example of analytic generalisation.

Many case studies, however, are restricted to examining the workings of one school, classroom, ward or group of people, and quite often the impact of some change upon them. These studies are frequently policy-driven, and the question of whether they can be taken as representative may be of considerable practical importance. Once again there are no hard and fast rules, and it is a matter of conceptual relevance and judgement. The more the study uncovers the workings of a process, the more confident we often are that it may be of more general application, because understanding a process gives us confidence that we know why some change or procedure has been effective. The better the theory we can build or develop, the more likely it is that we can apply the findings elsewhere. This raises again the now familiar issue that, when we do this, we are assuming that certain things will be held constant but we cannot be certain that we know what all these things are. Experience, previous studies and some theory tell us that a study carried out among a young group may well not apply to the elderly, that working-class groups may behave differently to middle-class ones, that the impact of a new baby on families with one child may be different from the impact of a first child. We do have some sense of what the boundary conditions are within which theories operate. We have to accept, however, that when we extend the findings of our evaluation to other situations, we can only be relatively certain of the consequences.

We should repeat what we said in the chapter on experiments. Our position must be clearly distinguished from one which holds that this kind of evaluative case study is strictly analogous to an experiment with a treatment and post-test measurement only. To the extent that this type of experiment is only interested in empirical, especially quantitative, findings and in relying entirely on the post-test measurement, the design is deeply flawed. Our position differs from the classic one in much of the literature on experimental designs, by our insistence that what is going on here must be judged by its theoretical grounding.

The choice of group and locale

This extended discussion of case studies has illustrated some very general dilemmas for research design. In one sense, all empirical research pays attention to a particular case, in the sense that its field of study is bounded by time and space. But something more is implied in the word 'case' than is implied by a phrase like 'unit of analysis': the term begs the question 'case of what?'. And the only way to answer that is through relevant theory. Thus whether a particular bank is a case of all banks, or all financial institutions, or all private companies, or all large bureaucracies, depends on the theory we are interested in investigating. There is nothing intrinsic in that bank *per se* that tells us what it is a case of. Looking at this the other way round, from the point of view of research design, we need to be guided by relevant theories when we are choosing cases – or, in other words, choosing locale and group. The choice may seem obvious: but we have to check carefully that it is, and we have to think laterally and imaginatively.

Sometimes, as we have pointed out, the group to be studied and the place in which it is to be studied are clearly defined by the research problem to be addressed. In evaluation studies this is generally the case, as the particular intervention we wish to look at applies only to specific people in a specific place. A new way of teaching reading may be tried out in a small group of schools, or we may be interested in the re-organisation of a hospital ward or commercial office. Questions may arise about the best comparator groups, or exactly how to design the work, but the people and the place are determined from the start.

Sometimes a researcher will have a very precise idea, from the outset, of the piece of research to be carried out. When this is so, the choice of group and locale is likely to be largely determined and the design problems will focus more on issues such as sample selection, the research instruments to be used, the expected comparisons, and so on.

Often, however, the researcher begins with a general curiosity about a little-researched topic, or is dissatisfied with some theory or explanation which is fairly widely accepted. The development of a design is then more of a cyclical process, whereby the best place to do the work and the group to be studied are considered, and alternatives are evaluated, imaginative comparisons made and the problems of control assessed. Then the impact on the exact problem to be investigated is considered. All good designs are compromises, and in this process the problem is refined, the group(s) and locale(s) reconsidered, alternative methods evaluated, some are adopted and some rejected, and the whole process continues until a satisfactory overall design emerges.

It is important to understand that research design always takes place under constraints. The amount of money available is limited, which is another way of saying that only a certain amount of time can be allocated to the work. The researcher may have good reasons for carrying out the work close to home, and problems of access make some groups very much harder to study than others. If the funding comes from a government department, then the choice of location may be constrained by the research contract. These factors influence researchers in their choice of problem. Most people who are interested in doing research are, at any one moment, aware of many more problems than they can tackle but which they might in principle wish to investigate. The particular problem they choose is of course mainly determined by a passionate wish to study some particular issue or research problem, but the choice between competing problems, or the approach to a particular problem, may be made because of the constraints under which the work is to be done. We shall take that much as given.

Are there, then, tried and tested ways of arriving at a good choice of group and locale once we have a general idea of the problem in hand? While individual researchers do undoubtedly develop repertoires for doing this, the general answer must be 'no'. The best we can do here is point the reader in the direction of some approaches.

The choice of a 'critical group' is one strategy. It can take many forms.

For instance, if we have reason to harbour serious doubts about the correctness or validity of some theory or account of a process, a good way of attempting to refute the theory is to design a piece of research in a locale and on a social group which is logically as favourable to one's opponents as possible. If by using this locale and by studying this group we can show that the theory is incorrect or the process is not taking place, we have good grounds for arguing that the theory or account of the process is incorrect. This refutation will of course only be as good as the logic behind the design.

One of the authors of this book was involved in what has become a classic example of this design, the Affluent Worker Studies (see Goldthorpe *et al.* (1969: 30–53) for the best account of the research design). In brief, the research set out to question the view, variously expressed in the literature, that certain sections of the British working class, as their material condition improved, had become middle class – the *embourgeoisement* thesis, as it became known. The logic of the study was to define, by reference to the literature making these claims, a group which one could argue would be so likely to be experiencing *embourgeoisement* that, if this group could be shown still to be working class, this made it highly improbable that the process was taking place anywhere in Britain. This logic can be applied in modified form to many studies. It is of course a relatively high-risk strategy. A social scientist using it has to be very confident that the theory under attack will indeed turn out to be incorrect. Otherwise the very logic of the design rebounds on the researcher. In the above example, had the group being studied turned out to be unequivocally middle class, then the general theory could not have been refuted but, more seriously, one would still not have been able to make any estimate of how widespread the phenomenon of *embourgeoisement* was. To show that a popular theory applies to the most favourable boundary conditions one can find will not cause much excitement. To show that it does not so apply will undoubtedly arouse interest.

Another approach involves the opposite kind of logic. Here, the researcher looks for a locale where the processes in which they are interested may be expected for conceptual reasons to be particularly salient. Let us give another example from our own ongoing work. Here the problem relates to national identity, which has become problematic throughout Europe in the late twentieth century. Issues of borders and frontiers have become more salient. The great bulk of the research, however, is on boundaries between states, especially those which are the subject of dispute, and around which and over which conflict is generated. The wish here was to study processes of identity formation, maintenance and transformation in relation to a border which, precisely because it is not the subject of conflict, and because it is a national border within a unitary state, is no hindrance to cross-border flows and social interaction, rendering its meaning fluid and problematic.

After reflecting on the borders within the United Kingdom, and various places on these borders, the research team came to the conclusion that nowhere in Britain provided a better locale in which to investigate such issues than Berwick-upon-Tweed, which lies two miles south of the Scottish border, halfway between Edinburgh and Newcastle: the only English town north of the Tweed, yet in a different country from Berwickshire. It is squeezed into the extreme north-eastern corner of England, with the North Sea on one side and the Scottish border on the other. The focus of the research was on how people on the border, in this somewhat contradictory location, construct, manage and make sense of their identity, both national and local.

Research designs are only as good as their underlying conceptual and empirical framework, and these designs are no exception. The Affluent Worker Studies can be attacked by arguing that for one reason or another the chosen town (Luton), or the three factories involved (Vauxhall Motors, SKF Ballbearings Co. or Laporte Chemicals), or the workers selected in these plants, are not the most likely to exhibit *embourgeoisement*. An alternative line of attack might be that the theory of *embourgeoisement* itself was not amenable to the kind of investigation undertaken. Similarly, the work in Berwick-upon-Tweed rests on conceptual arguments that national and local identities will be particularly contested and susceptible to change and variation under certain conditions. Theory and research design are intricately interwoven.

We have argued in this chapter that deciding what to study is an iterative process: it needs to be continually refined. We have suggested that all research studies are, in a sense, case studies, insofar as the empirical material they gather comes from a particular locale and group. But saying that is not enough: the choice of locale and group needs to be guided by the theory on which the whole research project is based. Another way of putting this is that we have to be able to answer the question: 'what is this locale and this group a case of?'. Answering this requires theory.

Fundamental to the use of theory to guide our choice of locale and group is comparison. The general approach to research design which we are advocating clearly implies that the researcher is always seeking original and illuminating comparisons of group or locale or both. It may be that the research problem leads fairly directly to a group to be studied and a place in which this is appropriately done. At this stage it is always worth considering whether one wishes to rely entirely on internal comparisons, within the group studied, or whether it might be better also to have a comparator group. It is at this point that the researcher reaches the limits of what can readily be taught. The message of this chapter, and indeed this book, is to encourage the search for exciting and illuminating, indeed unexpected, comparisons. But there is no formulaic way of approaching the imaginative and often lateral thinking required to come up with these comparisons. Often the best way to stimulate this imagination is by example. By studying how successful researchers have chosen illuminating groups and locales – such as in the examples cited in this chapter and elsewhere in the book – the new researcher can begin to develop an idea of how it is done.

5 To interview or not to interview

This book is about designing a good piece of research. The emphasis in this chapter is on obtaining an understanding of the nature and dynamics of various types of interview which can guide decisions on whether and how to use interviews in a particular research design. The questions the reader should keep in mind are: what are the issues of comparison and control which arise in different kinds of interview? And: could I obtain adequate information for my purposes together with better comparison and control using other methods?

In this chapter we discuss whether or not to include interviews in a research design, alternatives to interviewing, and the processes which are involved in the interview. It may at first seem strange to the reader that we should devote a considerable amount of space in this chapter to alternatives to interviewing. The point to be grasped is that whenever the researcher is thinking about using a particular kind of interview, it is wise to review both the advantages and the disadvantages, and to ask imaginatively whether information bearing on the issue could be obtained in some other way. This might be as an alternative or as an additional approach.

There are many different kinds of interview, each with its own advantages and disadvantages, which the researcher must consider carefully when deciding whether it is appropriate to use interviewing in a particular research design. We concentrate on the interview which is set up as an arranged interaction between the researcher(s) and others, be it very structured as in some surveys, or very unstructured. Interviews shade off almost imperceptibly into what we shall discuss later as fieldwork. Hard and fast distinctions are unhelpful, but we shall consider the conversations and other interactions which may take place in fieldwork in Chapter 7.

Researchers often build interviews into a research design almost automatically, because asking people questions seems on the face of it, and in the light of our experiences in everyday life, such an obvious way of finding out what they believe, think or feel. For similar reasons, inexperienced researchers feel that it is somehow easier and more natural to embark on a semi-structured interview programme than, for instance, to conduct and analyse a survey. It is perhaps tempting to think that anyone can do an interview, whereas it seems self-evidently obvious that survey analysis has to be learned. Such an assumption is entirely unwarranted.

We hope that reading this chapter will alert the reader to some of the issues of comparison and control in the interview. It is emphatically not a guide to carrying out a good interview or a cookbook on interview technique. There are many such books, some of which are listed in this book's guide to further reading, which should be consulted by people embarking for the first time on an interview programme, and this chapter makes no attempt to duplicate them. But a practical warning is in order. Reading such books is not enough. The research interview is not a straightforward conversation, and no one ever became even a competent interviewer, let alone a really good one, by reading books. It is essential for the beginner to do a number of pilot interviews, recorded either on audio or video tape, which can be discussed in detail with an experienced fieldworker. Good interviewing can be taught and can be learned.

To interview or not to interview?

When setting out to design a piece of research, those people who do tend to think immediately of talking to others and treat this as the research method *par excellence* should at least consider other alternatives. And similarly, those who do not generally think of using interviews might usefully ask themselves why this is so and whether talking to people would sometimes be worthwhile.

We have already pointed out that, when researchers are deciding on an appropriate research design and deciding how to collect their data, many of them immediately think of talking to people. But this is by no means a universal reaction. Economists tend to use data collected in other ways, although interviewing is being used increasingly in some branches of economics, especially micro-economics, famously by Hall and Hitch (1951) but also for instance by Brian Main (1993; 1994). Psychologists very frequently use other approaches, as do geographers. Historians, for obvious reasons, generally face one overpowering difficulty in talking to their subjects, much as they might wish so to do; those historians fortunate enough to be dealing with people still living have turned increasingly to forms of the interview, and oral history has become a lively branch of the discipline.

We take the view that social scientists could well be more imaginative in their choice of research designs and the methods used in them. Simply following the accepted paradigm in a particular discipline, while likely to lead to perfectly adequate research, is not the best way to be innovative. On the other hand, there is no point in adopting an innovative design just for the sake of it where there is a tried and tested approach which seems entirely suitable to the task in hand.

Our starting point, then, is to ask if researchers spend enough time thinking through whether the appropriate research design really does demand that they should talk to people. There is after all a wealth of other approaches. A good rule of research design might be never to choose the interview as the main research tool until all alternatives have been carefully and, above all, imaginatively considered. In many cases it is unlikely that interviews would then be discarded altogether, but the frequently lauded but less often achieved goal of 'data triangulation' would result.

'Triangulation of data' rests on the simple idea that several observations of a datum, a single piece of data, are better than one; the phrase implies that three are desirable. The idea comes from the technique of surveying land or establishing one's position on a map. If one takes two compass bearings on landmarks whose geographical position one knows accurately, one can draw on the map the bearings from these points, and where the two lines cross mark one's position. However, there is always some error in taking a bearing. If one takes bearings on three landmarks and draws the three bearings from these on the map then they will intersect and, because of error, form a small triangle. One hopes that the errors, and thus the triangle, will be small. What is certain, however, is that if the landmarks have been correctly identified, one's position will be somewhere in the small triangle formed by the intersection of the three lines. The idea of triangulating data, then, is that while each observation is prone to error, taking the three together will provide a more accurate observation.

Ever since the phrase was first used by Norman Denzin (1970), triangulation has become one of the mantras of empirical social science in much the same way as 'grounded theory' – frequently quoted and seldom examined. Yet the underlying idea is closely related to control. We are seeking a degree of certainty that the explanations we offer are indeed superior to competing explanations, and usually that, as discussed in Chapter 3, they are generalisable beyond the specific situation and group studied. Our confidence in our explanations is dependent on our confidence in the data, as well as on their theoretical grounding and logical structure.

There is what one might call a weak and a strong form of triangulation. The weak form is where we have multiple observations of something using the same method. When, for instance, we combine the responses to several questions in a survey into one index, this is what we are doing. The strong version is where several observations are made using different methods. If we are in the happy situation of being able to base part of an explanation on unstructured interview material, on documentary evidence and on the results of a survey, our confidence in our findings is likely to be greatly increased. Comparison of the data obtained from different methods can also play a part. If we compare survey data and qualitative interview material on a topic, or documentary evidence and what people say, there may be what at first sight look like inconsistencies. It is sometimes the case that these inconsistencies cannot be explained and the differing responses cannot be reconciled. In this situation the researcher has to make an informed and explicit decision whether to pursue the issue further or to place more reliance on one form of data than another. Sometimes, however, the discrepancy is itself revealing, and can be treated as a datum, as an observation to be explained. Differences between documentary evidence and what people say may relate to perceptions which are central to the problem in hand. Thus, as mentioned in Chapter 1, it is the discrepancy between the known statistics about crime and the fear of crime which gives the researcher a handle on the problem. Differences in crime statistics as reported to the police and those obtained in crime surveys reveal the underlying process of crime reporting, recording and classification. For instance, in general, more people report having been victims of crime in surveys than in crimes reported to the police (see for example Mayhew *et al.* 1993). Differences between survey material and qualitative interviews can sometimes be explained and used when it is realised that they arise from the meanings which are attributed to questions. For example, recent research by one of the authors and his colleagues on national identity used a formally structured question as well as extensive semi-structured interviewing (Bechhofer *et al.* 1999; McCrone *et al.* 1998). One respondent claimed to be British on the formally structured question. It became clear that this was the way he would present himself on most occasions because, having lived in Scotland for over fifteen years, he found it more acceptable to refer to himself as British, and in one sense had come to think of himself as British. Yet he had earlier clearly identified himself as English at a more personal level, and would no doubt present himself in this way when he thought it appropriate.

Alternatives to the interview

Our argument thus far is that it is as well to resist, in the first instance anyway, the almost automatic temptation to talk to people. Interviewing is by no means unproblematic. Although most people seem to enjoy well-conducted interviews on topics which interest them, response rates in surveys are falling. It is arguable that across the board social scientists invade people's privacy too often and demand too much of people's time. The interview is in some people's minds inextricably associated with officialdom, with interviews at Job Centres, assessments for social security and similar interactions. Even where the interview is to form part of the research design, the strong form of triangulation should be considered. In this section, we wish to highlight some of the many alternative ways of obtaining data which do not involve the researcher talking to people.

The analysis of documents and other kinds of text in already published or otherwise available form can be immensely rewarding, and there is an excellent discussion of this type of research in Scott (1990). Images such as advertisements (Goffman 1979), maps, film or photographs offer opportunities for imaginative analysis, providing the researcher resists the temptation to be seduced into believing that they represent 'the truth'. Film and photographs are a decidedly under-used form of data, although anthropologists have for a long time been active in this area (e.g Bateson and Mead 1942). The mass media – newspapers, magazines, radio and television programmes – have been seen both as objects of study in their own right and as texts describing or discussing events, and the views of individuals or groups. We discuss these two ways of approaching the media in Chapter 10. Letters (see for instance Hunter 1994; or the classic, Thomas and Znaniecki 1958) and diaries have been analysed both for the insights they provide specifically into their authors and for what they tell us about the lives of groups and classes at various times. An interesting account of the use between 1937 and 1950 of such materials by the social research organisation Mass Observation, and of its revival in 1981, is to be found in Sheridan (1993).

The analysis of such texts again involves a trade-off. We are not able as a rule to exercise any control over the way these documents are produced or what they contain, but on the other hand the texts, unlike transcripts of interviews, are not the result of a highly complex and inevitably somewhat artificial process of interaction. This emphatically does not mean that the process by which they were produced can be ignored. The reason we are going to discuss the interview method in more detail later in this chapter is to highlight the implications of the process for comparison and control. It is a basic contention of this book that whenever a piece of research is being designed, the researcher has to evaluate different designs involving different kinds of data. A good place to start that evaluation is the process by which data are generated.

A digression on history may be illuminating here. Existing collections of text are extremely rich, and historians, who usually have little choice but to use the written and other traces which have survived through time, are adept at extracting the best from them. Social scientists can learn much from the way in which historians, especially social historians, approach documentary material, and the lessons extend to data of other kinds. For instance, many of the questions which historians routinely ask of their data are relevant to interview material. The motives and intentions of the people who created the document, the reasons for the survival of this document rather than another, the audience for whom it was created, the possibility that it is a forgery, the way that meaning has changed over time: all these issues have their parallels in the study of interview transcripts and other material. Nor is the borderline between history and contemporary social science as hard and fast as might appear at first glance. The transcript of an interview carried out a month ago is an historical document.

Social scientists can get people to produce original documentary material rather than interviewing them. For instance, one does not have to depend on the happenstance production of and access to diaries. People can be asked to keep diaries of various kinds for a period of time. These may be used in a highly structured way. Time-budget studies involve the keeping of detailed diaries of the ways in which people use their time. It is usually done in a predetermined format, which allows systematic comparison and analysis (see Gershuny and Robinson 1988). When people record the things they have done in a systematic format at regular and fairly short intervals, they are much more likely to remember to include the smaller and less salient events, and to record the time taken more accurately. Such diaries are a far more reliable measure of the activities themselves than are the estimates obtained from surveys or other interviews. For instance, the discrepancies between what men and women tell interviewers about the gendering of activities and the data revealed by diaries are extremely revealing (see for instance Gershuny *et al.* 1994).

Diaries can also be used in a much less structured way. Elliott (1997) discusses the use of such diaries in qualitative health service research, and the discussion relates them also to the autobigraphical and biographical tradition referred to earlier. Just as people will sometimes tell strangers things they would not tell even quite close friends, they may record events, impressions and explanations which they find it difficult or painful to speak about to anyone, even the most sympathetic inteviewer.

Statistical data and data archives

In the United Kingdom we are fortunate in having some of the best official statistics obtainable anywhere, although sadly they have been reduced in scope somewhat in recent years. Nevertheless, it remains the case that there is a wealth of statistical information which has already been rigorously collected, often on very large samples, and which can be used by researchers. Until relatively recently the vast bulk of these data were only available by careful, time-consuming and, it must be admitted, tedious transcription from library or other printed sources. Much of this material has now been transferred to machine-readable media, and this process is accelerating rapidly with the advent of CD-ROM and the marketing of affordable CD-ROM readers either as add-on units or integrated within desktop computers. At the same time, global communication using the World Wide Web or Internet is growing exponentially, giving researchers rapid access to data all over the world.

Some of this aggregated statistical material has of course been collected using interview techniques or techniques of a similar kind. We can carry this one stage further by using in a research design interview data at the individual level, gathered by others but now available from archives for further analysis. Like everything else in research design, a decision to use these data and carry out secondary analysis is a matter of compromise. It can be an extremely efficient way of using much larger amounts of data than students, for instance, can usually obtain directly. The data are usually of a high standard, professionally collected and cleaned, and well documented. By using a number of such data sets, it may be possible to make more extensive comparisons between different groups than can any one researcher with limited resources. If, as is often the case, the data sets are large, the researcher can use statistical techniques giving high levels of control. The major disadvantage is obvious. The researcher has to make use of the data as collected. There will almost always be questions which were not asked but which seem central to the task in hand. With ingenuity it is possible to compensate up to a point for such gaps in the data. In the end, the researcher has to decide whether the advantages of using archived data are greater than the drawbacks.

The Census Office first made available in 1993, from a special unit at the University of Manchester, a sample of anonymised data at the individual level from the decennial Census of 1991. It has always been possible to obtain data at an aggregate level, but the protracted negotiations which led to the release of this data-set must be seen as a major breakthrough by everyone whose research project would benefit from the analysis of the rich if limited material collected in the Census.

In the United Kingdom, the Economic and Social Research Council (ESRC) funds a data archive at Essex University which has ever-growing quantities of available material (mainly, though not exclusively, survey data). As electronic communication improves and data transfer becomes more sophisticated, it is becoming ever easier to transfer material from the archive to one's own institution, and to analyse it by whatever means and on whatever computing platform one desires.

A further project which is only now in its formative stage is the proposal to create records of more qualitative material available from various archives. A great deal of interview material is collected each year of a semi-structured kind, and this for a number of reasons is seldom used for secondary analysis, unlike the survey-based material available from the data archive which is used extensively. Some of the difficulties surrounding qualitative data are indeed acute, because it is far more difficult to anonymise, and questions of confidentiality and ethics are complex and difficult to solve. Nevertheless, in principle there is a wealth of material here, and it is right that steps are being taken to make it more widely available.

Such secondary analysis of archived data, be it of a quantitative or qualitative kind, is indeed from the point of the view of the researcher doing it an alternative to carrying out interviews. The data themselves were of course originally obtained by interview, and this must always be kept in mind.

Non-reactive measures

Finally, there are measures which do not involve talking to people or intervening at all. These so-called non-reactive measures require careful thought, because while the researcher using them may not be intervening, the intervention may already have taken place, at one remove as it were. However, some very ingenious non-reactive measures have been used in research, and the book by Webb *et al.* (1966) is still well worth consulting as a source of ideas.

One ingenious example, which gives the flavour of the approach, was a study of a museum where the researcher wished to establish which exhibits were the most popular. The layout of this museum had not been changed for some considerable time, and a very good estimate of the situation was obtained by measuring floor wear around various exhibits. Similar techniques have been used to try to assess which library books have been consulted most frequently, and so on. These examples may be somewhat trivial, but the general idea that one can find out about the popularity of exhibits without necessarily asking people is an important one, and it is not difficult to see that some such measurement might have greater validity. Clearly, it would be far more difficult to find out *why* certain exhibits were popular in this way.

Another excellent example is the way in which the taken-for-granted nature of nationalism in everyday life has been discussed extensively and imaginatively in *Banal Nationalism*, a book by the social psychologist Michael Billig (1995). This book depends entirely on the use of non-reactive measures and the analysis of text. He draws our attention to the ways in which nationhood is constantly flagged in national life, flaggings whose 'unobtrusiveness arises, in part, from their very familiarity' (174) and how 'once one starts looking for flaggings, they seem to be ubiquitous' (175). One example is a literal flagging; the way in which national flags constantly appear, seldom consciously noticed, on buildings, commercial products, sporting platforms, and so on.

Degrees of structure in the interview

The point which has been laboured thus far is that most studies reach too readily for the technique in the social scientist's tool kit which comes most easily to hand. That is, talking to people. This is partly because talking to people is seen as an easy or natural thing to do, and in everyday life this is generally so. In research, talking to people is never the same as it is in everyday life, and it is far from being the case that it is the easiest, almost natural thing to do. One particular form of talking to people is regarded by the general public as the archetypal research approach. This is the survey interview, generally using a fairly highly structured schedule, but interviews are much more varied than that.

Lying behind a number of things already touched on in this chapter are two dimensions which affect the business of talking to people. One concerns the interview instrument itself. The interview schedule or frame may at one extreme be highly structured as a formal questionnaire, with every question completely determined, the alternative answers fixed, a rigid order of questions and all the introductions, and the words to be said between the questions, laid down. On the other hand, the interview instrument may be an interview guide of topics and a few crucial questions, or, under some circumstances, no listings of questions at all. We discuss structured questionnaires in detail in Chapter 6, but because students seldom come into contact with large-scale interview programmes, a brief digression is necessary. Questionnaires may be highly structured and still have built-in flexibility and be presented to the respondent in a relaxed way which conceals much of the rigidity. Large-scale surveys are usually conducted by a professional survey agency. The best agencies use a fairly large team of highly skilled and experienced interviewers. They are adept at presenting rigidly structured questions to respondents in a relaxed and spontaneous way, reading and re-reading the introductions to questions and the questions themselves consistently in each interview, and finding their way through often complex routings to ensure that the appropriate questions are asked of different groups of people; there might, for instance, be questions about the adequacy of the provision made for retirement asked only of the retired, or others about work not asked of the unemployed. We give some further examples in Chapter 6.

It is sometimes thought that the degree of comparison and control declines steadily from one end to the other of this continuum, running from the structured interview at one end to the unstructured interview at the other. It is undoubtedly easier to make statistical comparisons when a formal interview schedule is used, but comparisons may be far subtler and take account of finer shades of meaning in less structured interactions. This may be so even when the formal measure appears informative and produces convincing results. In recent times a formally structured question designed to investigate whether people feel British, more British than Scottish (or English), or vice-versa has been used widely and correlates well with various other variables (Brown *et al.* 1998: Ch. 9). Current research by one of the authors of this present volume and his colleagues, referred to earlier, shows that this occurs despite the underlying meanings of and reasons for making such claims varying greatly across different groups. For some purposes the greater access to meaning which we are granted at the unstructured end of the continuum may give us greater control. This will only be so, however, if the interviewing is carried out by the one researcher or at most a very small number of people, and this in turn restricts the sample size, which may in turn reduce control. As always, judgements have to be made when creating a research design about the trade-offs between different desirable outcomes. The particular trade-off just discussed is one of the reasons why, if resources permit, a powerful research design can be obtained by combining an initial formal survey with follow-up, intensive interviews with people selected from those already interviewed. Parry *et al.* in their book *Political Participation and Democracy in Britain* (1992) employ just such an approach. They did a general population survey, then a very similar survey on samples of political elites in six communities, and then followed this by interviews with these elites.

We turn now from the first dimension, concerned with the degree of structure of the interview schedule, to the second dimension affecting the business of talking to people, which relates to the way interviews are obtained and arranged. It runs from talking to people in highly formalised interview situations, through to participant observation in some kinds of field situation where the word interview becomes inappropriate and respondents tend to become informants.

If we take the two dimensions together we can see that they are inter-related. As a general rule, loosely structured instruments are the norm in highly participant field situations, and many social scientists would argue that unstructured interviews only work properly if the entire research process is set up and carried out informally, possibly over repeated inter-views. From this perspective the more formal interview situations require fairly structured schedules. These beliefs can, however, be inimical to good research design. Fieldwork of a highly participant, quasi-anthropological kind has frequently been constructively combined with formal methods such as a survey of the population of a village (Jeffery *et al.* 1989; Jeffery and Jeffery 1997). Semi-structured interviews can be successfully combined with the use of more formal approaches, such as scales in part of the interview (see for instance the details of the research summarised in Coxon and Davies (1986), where very sophisticated formal analysis was combined with interviews). By interviewing respondents twice, one can, as referred to earlier, combine the structure of a formal questionnaire with more unstructured questions guided by the results of the survey.

What has to be considered when setting up a research design and plan-ning research is the appropriateness of the general approach in terms of comparison and control. It simply is not the case that these things are self-evident, even though it is true that they are often taken as self-evident.

Types of interview

Inexperienced researchers when working out a research design often choose almost automatically the model of the face-to-face interview with one respondent, conducted by one interviewer, using a more or less struc-tured questionnaire. Such interviews are indeed the norm but, just as there are many kinds of data which do not require talking to people at all, there are some forms of interview which are less often used but about which the researcher should know something, as they may potentially provide the kind of information being sought together with sharper comparisons and higher degrees of control.

The focused interview

The focused interview was first used over fifty years ago (see Merton and Kendall 1946) and subsequently fell largely into disuse, although examples can be found in the literature from time to time, and the widely used focus group technique (see below) owes much to it. The technique may be used when it is decided to interview respondents about some situation in which it is known that they have been involved. A particular example is its use in disaster research. The researchers analyse as much information as they can obtain about the disaster from other sources, such as newspaper, radio and television accounts, available film and photographs, and so on. On the basis of this information, a fairly structured interview schedule is designed which can then be used with those who have been involved in the disaster in various ways. The idea is to provide a focus which can guide an interview on a very difficult topic and, in particular, that questions can be generated which really do enquire into the issues which the respondents saw as lying at the heart of the situation.

The non-directive or reflective interview

The totally non-directive or reflective interview is rarely appropriate in social science research as opposed to the clinical situation, but it can be used as a device during a generally more structured interview. The basic ideas are associated with the psychiatrist Carl Rogers, and the technique is that the interviewer does not ask questions but simply reflects back to the respondent the ideas and statements which the respondent generates. That the approach works is easily verified in any encounter, but a word of warning is in order. Because the respondent is being encouraged to develop the theme in any way which is meaningful to them, they can readily stray into ground which is both deeply personal and sensitive, particularly if the general topic of the interview is of this kind. Because this sort of technique is more applicable to just such topics, researchers intending to use it need advice and support from others with extensive experience of the pitfalls, and professional support. It is difficult to obtain control, and systematic comparison may be difficult.

Many years ago one of the authors was involved in a study which used a technique not identical but similar to this in an attempt to elicit people's images of the class structure (Goldthorpe *et al.* 1969: 145–56, Appendix C). In these interviews the approach was modified so as to avoid the kind of problems outlined in the previous paragraph. This section of the schedule was introduced by a very general question: 'People often talk about there being different classes. What do you think?'

Subsequent questioning used the ideas which the respondent put forward (and no others) in order to pursue the issue further and attempt to build up a picture of the class structure as the respondent saw it. At no point were new ideas or concepts suggested to the respondent, but rather their own ideas were reflected back to them in a manner which caused them to continue developing their thoughts for the interviewer.

Group interviewing and the focus group

There is a growing literature on group interviewing, where several respondents are interviewed together. As was mentioned earlier, the interview, the process of talking to a respondent, while it appears entirely natural is in fact a somewhat artificial situation. Group interviews can sometimes move closer to a social situation as it is more generally experienced. They are economical in terms of researcher time and thus cost. Group interviews were not widely used until relatively recently, when a particular form of group interview – the focus group – came to be used very widely in market research and in the management of political affairs.

Interestingly, the focus group (see for instance Morgan 1997; Stewart 1990) owes its origins to a much earlier phase of social research and is associated with Paul Lazarsfeld, the distinguished American methodologist, who was also much involved in market research. This is almost certainly the route by which it came to be taken up in that area, but it was not until very recently used in social science research more generally. This technique involves bringing a group of people together and conducting a very lightly structured interview with them around some particular focused topic. It has that in common with the focused interview discussed earlier. Successful use of focus groups requires a good understanding of the dynamics of a group, and it is unlikely that researchers could use it satisfactorily without some prior training in the technique.

The use of multiple interviewers

Finally, among unusual or less used interviews is the use of multiple interviewers. Effectively, this is the reverse of the group interview because here there is one respondent and two interviewers. Just as the group interview is relatively cheap, this is costly, and the advantages it undoubtedly offers for certain kinds of interview have to be balanced against the costs. The approach can produce much better comparison and control, because it allows one interviewer to concentrate on how the respondent's comments relate to the theoretical and conceptual interests of the research and what has been said by other respondents. The technique, if the interview is not being recorded, is for the interviewers to alternate, with one taking notes and reflecting on what is being said while the other one speaks, and then switching roles. If the interview is being recorded, the interviewer who is not speaking at the time can concentrate entirely on observing and thinking about the next line of enquiry. It is only appropriate when interviewing certain types of people, because being confronted by two interviewers is a somewhat intimidating situation. The technique is probably most successful, therefore, in situations where those being interviewed either are familiar with the interview situation or alternatively are extremely confident of their views and perhaps their position in society. Interviews with elites or particularly powerful people are situations in which the technique has been successfully used (Bechhofer *et al.* 1984).

The interview process

We return now to the question of the interview process in general. If we wish to think about how one achieves comparability and control, it is necessary to realise that the interview is neither an arcane research process nor quite as straightforward as it seems. What we are trying to do in the interview is to formalise and use in a research design a fundamental part of the business of social interaction in day-to-day life. This is why the phrase 'talking to people' rather than 'carrying out an interview' seems attractive in that it suggests the normality of the interview. And yet, looked at more analytically, the research interview is seen to be highly artificial, not normal at all. We are effectively studying social interaction and social structure by using a special version of a fundamental building block of that social interactive process. There is a reflexivity about the interview process which is seldom thought about explicitly. If interviews are to be used well in a research design and are to achieve their object, it is necessary to understand the dynamics of the interview, and to appreciate that they can never be normal conversations even at the most unstructured end of the spectrum. Even when using the most loosely structured approach, the researcher is carrying out the interviews for a purpose, and with a view to obtaining information about something bearing on the research project in hand. In the course of the interview, implicitly or explicitly, the researcher is comparing what is being said with what other persons have said, assessing whether it is something new or something which supports other information. Even if the interviewer is asking the minimum of questions and is allowing the respondent to range very widely, virtually all interviews are bounded in the sense that not everything the respondent might wish to discuss will be of interest to the researcher.

The interview is an interactional process, an encounter, with three major characteristics. First, it has shared interactional rules. Second, it is generally carried out between strangers. And third, it is frequently a one-off affair. All conversations have shared interactional rules, but they are not precisely the same as those governing the interview. Some conversations are between strangers, but these are by no means the dominant form of social interaction. And by the same token, most conversations are not one-off affairs. Those which are tend to be restricted to fairly formal and sometimes ritualised situations, and this is an invaluable insight into the interview as a research tool.

That interviews and conversations are different activities is fundamental to the method. There are particular social norms and values governing the interview. It is this that allows the researcher to steer the semi-structured interview in a way which would be inappropriate in a normal conversation, and structure it even more rigidly in a survey interview. It is in these ways that it becomes possible to make comparisons and achieve control.

In what one might call the classic interview, the interviewer, in exchange for information of an honest kind, listens, does not argue or deny the respondent's views, is not shocked or pleased, and does not contradict or hassle the respondent. In exchange for being listened to in this rather unusual way the respondent provides the interviewer with the information that is being sought. It is regarded as a trade-off which satisfies both parties. Now, quite obviously there are some fundamental issues here. What is meant by honest information, and can it be traded in this way? There have been some very serious challenges to this classic model of the interview, for example from feminist authors, in that some researchers see the interview as necessarily much more of a shared experience rather than one in which the interviewer is simply a passive receiver of information (see for instance Finch 1993; Oakley 1981; Reinharz 1992; Smith 1987). In the archetypal interview, three broad issues arise.

First, the interviewer may have expectations of the respondent in terms of what the respondent knows, believes, feels, and so on. This is a normal aspect of social interaction. If we did not have expectations of those with whom we interact, life would be a great deal more difficult. We would be much more often surprised by what we hear and it would be difficult to conduct affairs with any degree of certainty.

In the research interview, however, the question is how these expectations affect the data which are collected, whether one can control these expectations, and so forth. In the 'classic' model, the interviewer is expected to be a recorder of neutrally elicited information. The interviewer's expectations of the respondent are then seen as a possible source of systematic response errors or of non-response. The interviewer is thus required to reduce these expectations to a minimum, to try to approach the respondent with a completely open mind. This issue is centrally related to the question of control.

It is tempting, especially for people new to interviewing, to think of these expectations which the interviewer brings to the interview as prior expectations, perhaps generated by prejudice or stereotyping. Just as important, however, are the expectations which are generated in the process of an interview programme. After a while, researchers come to expect respondents to say certain things and fail to pick up new responses; in highly structured interviews they have been known to hear one thing but mark the wrong response on the schedule. The subtler the deviation from the customary response, the easier it is to miss. This process of habituation can produce a false sense of control, a belief that conclusions are well grounded when they are not.

Second, these expectations which the interviewer may have are mirrored by those of the respondent, who may have expectations of the interviewer. It is obviously impossible to stop the respondent having these expectations, or in any way to set up the interview in a manner requiring or even requesting the respondent not to have such expectations, but it is, according to the 'classic model', possible up to a point to manipulate them.

The question is whether the interviewer can, or should, standardise the cues that are given off, thus increasing control, and if this is possible in principle, how it can be done in practice. This is by no means a straightforward issue. This can be seen by considering for a moment the question of dress. If the interviewer dresses in the standard manner expected of interviewers – shall we say neatly, soberly and without any unusual features – what is the effect on the respondent? Although it is true that all respondents are being offered a standard stimulus as it were, the way different respondents react to it will vary from social grouping to social grouping. For example, different people react differently to someone in a suit. In many working-class areas, the wearing of a suit is synonymous with authority or officialdom, and may be treated with suspicion. Different people react differently to what they see as very casual dress or hairstyle or other aspects of appearance. Thus, even if one wishes to standardise the effect in order to achieve greater control, it may be the case that wearing the same clothes in all situations does not succeed in this aim.

Third, the respondent may have beliefs about the expectations that the interviewer has of them. In other words, even if the interviewer has no expectations at all, the respondent may believe that they do have such expectations and that certain kinds of view or opinion or response are expected. Can one then successfully reassure respondents that the interviewers do not have such expectations? Should one even attempt so to do, obviously risking being thought to protest too much? Interviews have become commonplace in people's lives, arguably too much so, and such reassurance seems to be accepted by respondents as articulating quite well-understood unwritten rules. This to some extent standardises the interview and leads to greater control. But acting in this way undoubtedly increases and emphasises the artificiality of the interaction which is taking place. In a normal conversation one does not generally reassure the person to whom one is talking that one does not have such beliefs, and if one did it is doubtful whether one would be believed.

The crux of the issue is whether, in obtaining good comparison and control, meaning changes and validity is lost. If this is the case then other kinds of research design, such as the use of fieldwork, may get round these problems. In turn they present difficulties of their own, as is discussed later in this book. Research design is always a matter of informed compromise.

6 Structured questionnaires

If interviews are – as we argued in Chapter 5 – unavoidably fluid because they are a species of social interaction, structured questionnaires are a means of trying to control that uncertainty. They are a very common method of social research; indeed, the average person in the street probably thinks of them as *the* method of social research, the structured question-naire handled by an interviewer with a clipboard. They are especially common in large-scale social research for reasons that we will come to.

There are three parts to this chapter:

- What structured questionnaires are, and what their strengths are.
- The technical problems associated with structured questionnaires: that is, problems that can be addressed within the broad framework of structured questionnaires.
- What can be concluded about the validity of this technique, given all the problems and advantages.

Strengths of structured questionnaires

To give an initial flavour of what this kind of questionnaire involves, consider an example from a large-scale survey that depended on a good-quality structured questionnaire – the British Election Survey of 1992, carried out to coincide with the general election of that year (Heath *et al.* 1994). Figure 6.1 shows a small part of the questionnaire. The point of this illustration is not the details, but the overall structure and style. The page shows the typical kinds of instructions that are given to interviewers. Instructions are in capitals; things which she has to read out are in ordi-nary sentence style. (We refer to interviewers as 'she' in this chapter, because in practice they nearly always are in this kind of research.) For example, in Question 2b, the interviewer has to read out exactly what is written: first, 'Which *daily morning* newspaper do you read *most* often?',

2a. Do you regularly read one or more <u>daily morning</u>
newspapers?

Yes	1 ASK b.
No	2 GO TO Q4.

IF YES (CODE 1) AT a.

b. Which <u>daily morning</u> newspaper do you read <u>most</u> often? And
which do you read <u>next most</u> often?

ONE CODE IN EACH COLUMN BELOW

	Most often	Next most often
(Scottish) Daily Express	01	01
Daily Mail	02	02
Daily Mirror/Record	03	03
Daily Star	04	04
The Sun	05	05
Today	06	06
Daily Telegraph	07	07
Financial Times	08	08
The Guardian	09	09
The Independent	10	10
The Times	11	11
The Scotsman	12	12
The Glasgow Herald	13	13
Press and Journal	14	14
Other Scottish/Welsh/regional or local <u>daily morning</u> paper (WRITE IN) _____ _____	15	15
Other (WRITE IN) _____	16	16
None	-	00

Figure 6.1 Example of structured questions from questionnaire for the 1992
British Election Survey

Source: Heath *et al.* 1994: 312.

and then she notes the reply in the first column; second, 'And which do
you read *next most* often?', the reply being noted in the other column. So
if the respondent reads, most frequently, the *Daily Mail*, then the interviewer will put a circle round the 02 in the first column, and if the next

most frequent is, say, the *Daily Express*, the second column will have a circle round 01. The point of all this is that it is absolutely standard. The interviewer would have one of these forms for each of the people that she was interviewing, and would follow the same rules for each of them.

Indeed, so standardised has this kind of interviewing become that the interviewer can now be instructed by a laptop computer what to ask, and can enter the responses directly into the computer. This speeds up the subsequent transfer of data from the interviewer's record of the responses to the computer package on which the statistical analysis of the survey will be based. The 1997 British Election Survey was done in this way. There was a sequence of questions which was almost exactly the same as those shown in Figure 6.1, but they appeared, one by one, on the interviewer's screen instead of on a sheet of paper. She entered responses on that screen, and the computer stored them. This technique is called Computer Assisted Personal Interviewing (CAPI) or – where appropriate – Computer Assisted Telephone Interviewing (CATI). Of course, the gains it offers are offset by the time taken to program the computer.

Structured written questionnaires can be administered either by interview or by post. For postal surveys they are, in fact, the only option realistically available. In other words, you have to have clear instructions with relatively simple questions and relatively straightforward ways of answering them. You cannot really expect people to write essays in reply to postal questionnaires (although we return to this point later). However, they are also very useful in interview surveys.

The first advantage for research design of this highly structured approach to questionnaires is efficient use of time. Time to do the research might seem to be a trivial matter if you are just embarking on a project, but that is not how it seems once you get going. Time is especially important for large-scale surveys that are being paid for commercially or by some grant-giving organisation (such as the UK Economic and Social Research Council which sponsored the Election Surveys). When budgets are limited, they have to be spent efficiently. So it is very important to be able to ask a very simple question – 'Which paper do you read?' – and then go directly to the answer and move quickly to the next question. It is also important that the interviewer (or, in a postal survey, the respondent) gets clear instructions on the way to proceed through this questionnaire. For example, Question 2a in Figure 6.1 asks 'Do you regularly read one or more daily morning newspapers?'. If the respondent says 'No' to this, then the interviewer immediately skips to Question 4 (not shown in the Figure) and omits Question 2b (about *which* paper) completely. This is even easier with computed-aided interviewing: in the 1997 Election Survey, if the answer to the preliminary question was 'No', then the computer simply did not show the question with the list of newspapers, jumping automatically to the next question in the sequence.

Moreover, because each interviewer asks exactly the same question, the training of interviewers can be done in groups, and that too is very efficient. Typically, with large-scale survey organisations, there would be regional training sessions. This is because, to do interviewing effectively, you have to have interviewers based locally, who know local accents, local words, local patterns of work (important for knowing when to catch people in), etc. For example, the training session in Glasgow would be for perhaps twenty interviewers, who would probably be dealing with the whole of West-Central Scotland. So structured questionnaires use time efficiently in the training of interviewers as well as in the conduct of the interview.

The second advantage of structured questionnaires for research design is that the questions are standardised with a common and transparent meaning – or at least every effort is made to ensure this. So, in a survey which uses interviewers, they do not have to interpret the questions. In a postal survey, the aim is that the respondents should, as far as possible, take the same meaning from the questions. (We look later at some of the things which have to be taken into account in trying to achieve this standardisation.) The interviewer is then just the mouthpiece of the social science researcher. Much of the training of interviewers is an attempt to get them to be neutral in relation to the questions, to read out what is on the paper (or on the screen), and on each occasion to do it with exactly the same intonation and emphasis. The interviewer also has to be trained to deal in standard ways with queries from the respondents. Even if you yourself are doing all your own interviews, it is important to teach yourself to be neutral and standard in this sense.

A third advantage of structured questionnaires is that they are ideal for statistical descriptions, and so they are ideal for asking about factual matters. For example: What is your occupation? What is your age? How many educational qualifications do you have? What newspapers do you read? This is why censuses tend to be conducted in these ways because censuses are, in most countries, exclusively concerned with facts of that sort.

The technique of standardised questionnaires has emerged in response to some of the doubts that there might be about the validity of the inferences drawn on the basis of a research design that rests on questionnaires and on interviewing. This may sound slightly paradoxical. Formal questions are often criticised for imposing a cognitive world on the people being interviewed: that is, a view of the world that is shaped by social science theories more than by common experience (a criticism to which we return at the end of the chapter). But it can be argued that the reason for using these structured questionnaires is actually the opposite. By standardising the questions we reduce to a minimum, we hope, the role of the researcher or of the interviewer, and so the variation in meaning between respondents is entirely due to these respondents themselves.

And the point of all this is to make comparison easier. We want to compare one group of respondents to another group of respondents, and we want to know that any differences in the response between these two groups is due to some characteristic of these respondents rather than to some way in which they were asked the question. The point about factual questions simply illustrates that valid comparisons are easier when opinions do not intrude.

Problems with structured questionnaires

Even the greatest enthusiasts for standardised questionnaires would nevertheless recognise that there are problems with them, and a lot of research and practical experience has gone into trying to cope with the problems. In the terms we have been using in this book, the problems are about the validity of the comparisons we can make.

One way of understanding how the problems arise is to look at some of the things that psychologists have written about the ways in which people respond to standardised questionnaires. There are many models of response, but the one in Figure 6.2 is fairly typical. It comes from research by Cannell *et al.* (1981: 393) at the University of Michigan, the pre-eminent academic centre in the United States for social survey research. (The model is assessed by Sykes and Morton-Williams (1987).)

---

1   Comprehension of the question.
2   Cognitive processing to arrive at an answer, including:

   i   assessments and decisions concerning the information needed for an accurate answer;
   ii   retrieval of cognitions (attitudes, beliefs, experiences, facts);
   iii organisation of the retrieved cognition and formulation of the response on this basis.

3   Evaluation of the response in terms of its accuracy.
4   Evaluation of the response in terms of other goals (e.g. self-image, desire to please the interviewer).
5   Giving the response judged as accurate and based on adequate processing.

Figure 6.2 Cannell *et al.*'s model of response to structured questionnaires

The problem that is being explored here is: what is the process that goes on in a person's mind after they have been asked a question and before they utter an answer? First of all the person has to understand the question, both in the rudimentary sense of understanding the words that are used, and in the sense of understanding what the question means. For example, a question about how the respondent would vote in an election requires understanding of what elections are, what parties do, and so on. Then, second, there has to be cognitive processing, in other words thinking. People have to think about the question and that includes, Cannell *et al.* suggest, three possible things. There are decisions concerning what information is needed – 'What do I have to know in order to be able to answer this question?'. In our example of newspaper readership in Figure 6.1, the respondent has to know what newspaper they read. Then there is searching for that information. So the respondent has to remember which newspaper they read. Then there has to be a coherent response. Third in the model, the respondent has to decide whether the response that has come to mind is accurate. Fourth, there go through the respondent's mind what we as social researchers might think of as irrelevant considerations – for example, 'Is what I am about to say going to be acceptable to me in terms of my self-image or my desire to please the interviewer or, indeed, my desire to annoy the interviewer?'. These are sometimes called 'social desirability' effects. Famously, for the 1992 general election in the UK, it is now thought that people who were going to vote Conservative felt that that was a rather shameful thing to do. They did not say so, and the opinion polls underestimated the Conservative vote (Market Research Society 1994; O'Muircheartaigh and Lynn 1997). And then, finally, the respondent actually says what they have concluded from this process.

This is a model, not a description: the processes are not supposed to happen sequentially in the way that we have gone through them here, and respondents might cycle round the stages before deciding on a final answer. It is one way in which psychologists have analysed people's thought processes as they answer questions in a survey. It is not the only model, but it contains important features of many of the models that have been offered. The point that matters for our purposes is not so much the detail of this particular model as the light which it casts on our role as researchers. The model reminds us that our capacity to structure responses by means of research design is actually rather limited. We can contribute to step 1: we can try to make sure that the questions are clear (as we will see). And perhaps we can do something about step 4: we can try to make people feel at ease about giving socially unacceptable answers. But there is not much we can do about steps 2, 3 and 5. For example, in an interview lasting three-quarters of an hour, we cannot train people in memory skills, and with postal questionnaires we can do little to prompt their memory. This is the reason why most of the writing about how to design standard-ised questionnaires concentrates almost entirely on step 1, how to devise questions which are easily understood. This is extremely important, but we must always remember that designing questions addresses only some of the very complex things that are going on inside the respondent's mind.

So, what can be done to reduce the extent to which the question struc-ture and wording interfere with our capacity to make valid comparisons? Here, in fact, massive amounts have been written because there are many things which can be done. You can sit in your study and fiddle around with a questionnaire, and so it appears easy. A lot of this could be thought of as being common sense – writing clear words or speaking in clear ways. But there are also problems to do with whose common sense this is, a point we come to in the last section of this chapter. Some examples of contrasting common sense will come up as we go on.

When discussing the design of individual questions, it is quite useful to have a basic distinction in our mind between factual questions and opinion questions. An example of a factual question is:

How much wine did you consume last week?

By 'factual' is meant not whether the *answer* is factual – is true – but rather whether there is in principle a true answer. So the example does have a single true answer, however intrinsically difficult it might be to find out what that is. An example of an opinion question is the following, used in the 1996 British Social Attitudes Survey (Jowell *et al.* 1997):

Looking back over the past year or so, would you say that Britain's economy has got stronger, got weaker, or has it stayed about the same?

Opinion questions sometimes pose as factual questions, as this example shows. It purports to ask the respondent about a state of affairs. But in fact, of course, the research interest lies not in whether this is true, whether the British economy did improve, but rather in what the range of opinion of the population is on this question. There are indeed factual issues bearing on the question, but the respondent's knowledge of them is not the primary interest.

So factual questions sometimes appear to be opinion questions, and opinion questions to be factual questions, but the distinction is useful to maintain because it tells us about the kind of data we will collect. Some surveys are designed primarily to get factual information. In the UK, almost all government surveys are factual surveys. The Family Expenditure Survey, the General Household Survey and the Labour Force Survey, as well as the census, consist almost entirely of factual questions. So too do many important research surveys, even where opinions also are of interest. For example, the British Election Survey contains many factual questions – how respondents voted, which newspapers they read, and so on. One particular kind of factual question which is nearly always asked is the 'classification question', mainly to distinguish amongst different groups of respondents so that you can compare the responses for these different groups. Examples include asking about the respondent's gender, social class, age, region of origin, ethnicity, and so on. Information about these matters also sometimes allows us to assess the extent to which the sample is representative, by comparing the distribution in the sample with known information about the population. For example, if we find that 52 per cent of a sample of the general population of Britain is female, then we know that, so far as gender is concerned, the sample is representative of the population, because that is also the proportion of the population which is female. These questions are often called 'face sheet questions', although this is misleading because frequently they are asked at the end of the process, it being thought to be boring for people to be asked facts about themselves.

Some of the points to be considered about designing question wording apply to factual questions, but most of them are more relevant to opinion questions. Generally, first, it is thought that long questions produce better responses. This may seem paradoxical but the point is that it allows people to reflect: it makes them feel that the questions are serious, that they are worth thinking about. It appears from various experiments that have been done that a longer question reduces the effect of social desirability, that people seem to be willing to give more truthful answers to longer questions than to shorter questions. Longer questions also appear to improve people's recall, in that they allow them to think about the matter in different ways (Groves 1989).

However, if you are going to ask a long and complex question, it has to be broken down into briefer segments to indicate how people are to go through it. Figure 6.3 shows an example. It comes from the 1992 British Election Survey again, and is a question seeking opinions about the highly complex issue of taxes and government services, and also opinions about the various political parties' views on these matters. The interviewer would read out what appears in the box against Question A36, and would also show a card with this on it to the respondent. While the interviewer is doing this, she is showing the scales – also on the card – to the respondent. The interviewer then reads, in turn, each of the questions in the

A36.	Please look at this page.
	Some people feel that governments should put <u>up taxes a lot and spend much more on health and social services</u>; these people would put themselves in Box A. (POINT)
	Other people feel that governments should <u>cut taxes a lot and spend much less on health and social services</u>; these people would put them in Box K. (POINT)
	And other people have views somewhere <u>in-between</u>, along here (POINT LEFT A-F) or along here (POINT RIGHT K-F).

a.   In the first row of boxes, please tick whichever box comes closest to <u>your own</u> views about taxes and government spending.

		f. CODING: RING ONE IN EACH COLUMN				SCOTLAND ONLY
	Now where do you think the Conservative and Labour parties stand:	a. Own views	b. Conser-vative	c. Labour	d. Liberal Democrat	e. SNP
b.	First, the Conservative Party. In the next row of boxes, please tick whichever box you think comes closest to the views of the <u>Conservative Party</u>?	A=01 B=02 C=03 D=04	A=01 B=02 C=03 D=04	A=01 B=02 C=03 D=04	A=01 B=02 C=03 D=04	A=01 B=02 C=03 D=04
c.	Now in the next row please tick whichever box you think comes closest to the views of the <u>Labour Party</u>?	E=05 F=06 G=07	E=05 F=06 G=07	E=05 F=06 G=07	E=05 F=06 G=07	E=05 F=06 G=07
d.	And now, please tick whichever box you think comes closest to the views of the <u>Liberal Democrats</u>?	H=08 I=09 J=10 K=11	H=08 I=09 J=10 K=11	H=08 I=09 J=10 K=11	H=08 I=09 J=10 K=11	H=08 I=09 J=10 K=11

IN SCOTLAND ONLY

e.	Now tick whichever box you think comes closest to the views of the <u>Scottish National Party</u>?					
	Left of A	=12	=12	=12	=12	=12
	Right of K	=13	=13	=13	=13	=13
	Don't know	=98	=98	=98	=98	=98

f.   ASK ALL

Now please tell me the <u>letters</u> of the boxes you ticked in each row, starting with the first row

RING CODES IN GRID AS APPROPRIATE

INTERVIEWER: You may change any code already ringed if, on reflection, a respondent wants to change his or her mind. Ensure that final entries are clear on grid. If asked you may confirm that letter F is the middle box.

Figure 6.3 Example of complex question from questionnaire for the 1992 British Election Survey

Source: Heath *et al.* 1994: 320.

left-most column (labelled a to f); for the time being, the interviewer pays no attention to the grid on her own questionnaire. The first question asks 'Which view comes closest to your own?' (part a), and the respondent has to mark a point on the scale A to K. And then, beyond that, the respondent is asked to place the Conservative Party on that scale (part b), then the Labour Party (part c), then the Liberal Democrats (part d) and then, in Scotland, the SNP (part e). The respondent marks all these answers on the page given to him or her by the interviewer: this sheet has the response categories A to K. The interviewer then (in part f) asks the respondent to read out the letter chosen for each part of the question, and the interviewer writes the answers on the grid in the questionnaire.

So this is a complex question with four or five dimensions of response. Clearly, this has allowed scope for a lot of thought about the nature of political philosophy, policy, trust in government, and many related things (and the instruction to the interviewer at the foot allows the respondents to change their mind). In order to get any kind of meaningful answer at all, it has had to be broken down into steps and dimensions. But it could be argued that the breaking down of the question has also over-simplified it.

The second point about question wording is clarity. It is obviously important to avoid ambiguity. A very obvious case of ambiguity would be wording such as 'Do you like travelling by train or bus?'. This is ambiguous because it could mean, on the one hand, 'Do you like travelling by train or do you like travelling by bus?' or, on the other hand, 'Do you like travelling by train or bus as opposed to by aeroplane?'. This example may seem too blatant, yet when you are immersed in a project it is remarkably easy to miss such apparently obvious ambiguities. But more subtle potential ambiguities are certainly more difficult to notice, and there can be few questions that do not potentially contain some ambiguity in some contexts. In the example we looked at in Figure 6.1, what is meant by 'read'? How does someone answer who reads the *Daily Mirror* every day for the sports coverage but the *Guardian* once every couple of days for other news?

The next point is that you have to consider the language level. This is not straightforwardly a matter of using simple language all the time, because simple language can seem patronising, and some of the difficulties arise in finding a level of language that is appropriate to the people who are being questioned. For example, asking about 'taxation policy' might be appropriate in a survey of the general population, while the term 'fiscal policy' could be more appropriate for a more specialist group. Rarely nowadays do researchers make the kind of mistake which Moser and Kalton (1985: 321) quote from the UK Enquiry into Family Limitation that was conducted in 1949. It asked:

Has it happened to you that over a long period of time, when you neither practised abstinence nor used birth control, you did not conceive?

The unfortunate respondents had to answer 'Yes' or 'No'.

Even if the language is at an appropriate level, you still have to think about how easy it will be for the respondents to get hold of the necessary information. For example, if you ask people how they voted at the last general election their memories will be quite poor, especially for political parties that were nowhere near gaining power. In the 1992 British Election Survey, only 14 per cent of respondents who could recall their vote said that they had voted for the Liberal/SDP Alliance at the previous general election five years earlier, even though in reality 23 per cent had voted for the Alliance. This discrepancy was not because the 1992 survey was itself biased: unlike the opinion polls, it got the 1992 result almost right (Heath *et al.* 1994). Nor was the recall of the 1987 vote uniformly poor for all parties: the discrepancy was a 3 per cent underestimate in the recall of the 1987 Labour vote and a 7 per cent overestimate in the recall of the 1987 Conservative vote. One way of getting around the problem of memory is to ask people to keep a diary – as discussed in Chapter 5 – or to interview the same people on several occasions; but of course that makes the survey much more expensive and lengthy. This kind of approach is now part of the British Election Surveys (Heath *et al.* 1994).

Moreover, people feel obliged to provide answers to questions even when they have little knowledge on which to base their response. This can be detected when the same topic is asked about in different ways, highlighting different aspects of it in the wording of the question. One example of this is reported by Curtice and Jowell (1998: 67–8), concerning attitudes in Britain to using proportional representation for elections to the UK parliament. The first version of the question asked in the British Election Survey of 1997 is:

> How much do you agree or disagree with this statement? Britain should introduce proportional representation so that the number of MPs each party gets matches more closely the number of votes each party gets.

The second version is:

> Some people say we should change the voting system to allow smaller parties to get a fair share of MPs. Others say we should keep the voting system as it is to produce effective government. Which view comes closest to your own?

In the first version, 49 per cent of people favoured reform and 16 per cent opposed it. In the second version, 35 per cent were in favour and 60 per cent were opposed. Presumably the reason for the difference is that the first version associates proportional representation with votes being meaningful, whereas the second associates it with ineffective government. People do not carry around in their heads all the arguments concerning this complex issue, and so are susceptible to changes in wording which make particular arguments prominent.

Although all the points made so far about question wording apply equally to factual and opinion questions, there are some special difficulties with opinion questions. It is usually better to avoid leading questions. However, some people should know better than their practice suggests. For example, in 1991, the Committee of Vice-Chancellors and Principals of UK universities commissioned the survey organisation MORI to ask this question (see the *Guardian*, 4 February 1992: 23):

> Money provided by the Government for teaching university students has not kept pace with the increased number of students at university. This means that the amount of the money for teaching each student is falling. What do you think the Government should do?

Now, whatever your views may be about government cutbacks, this is not an unbiased question, and so obviously produces useless results.

That example is fairly extreme. But guarding against subtle biases is not easy. Consider this example, from the 1986 British Social Attitudes Survey (Jowell *et al.* 1986), about taxation versus government spending:

> It has been suggested that the National Health Service should be available only to those with lower incomes. This would mean that contributions and taxes could be lower and most people would then take out medical insurance or pay for health care. Do you support or oppose this idea?

Now try changing the middle sentence by simply substituting 'but' for 'and', so that it reads

> This would mean that contributions and taxes could be lower but most people would then take out medical insurance...

This apparently minor change could alter the whole tenor of the question. The point is not that either the 'and' or the 'but' version is perfect, but that you cannot avoid one of them. Using 'and' implies that there is no necessary disadvantage from private medical insurance; using 'but' implies that there is a disadvantage. Either way, the question cannot help implying a certain political framework. So this issue of the biasing effects of question wording can be as much a matter for how you interpret the data as for design, although it is preferable to remove as much bias as possible at the design stage.

A second point about opinion questions is that people may not have thought about their opinions at all. They may have latent opinions and the question might partly be forming their opinions. So a question implicitly sets an agenda. Here is an example from the British Social Attitudes Survey (Jowell *et al.* 1986) relating to the actions which people say they would take if they disagreed with a proposed piece of legislation:

> Suppose a law was now being considered by parliament, which you thought was really unjust and harmful. Which, if any, of the things on this card do you think you would do?

- Contact my MP
- Speak to influential person
- Contact a government department
- Contact radio, TV or newspaper
- Sign a petition
- Raise the issue in an organisation that I already belong to
- Go on a protest or demonstration
- Form a group of like-minded people
- None of these
- Don't know

Providing a list was unavoidable in order to get a manageable set of answers. But doing that has also fixed the scope of the answers, and it has also set a context of the kind of things that you do in a society that is a functioning parliamentary democracy. For example, it does not say here 'Go out and shoot the minister responsible', or 'Organise an insurrection'.

A third point about opinion questions concerns their structure. A distinction is often drawn between open questions and pre-coded questions. Pre-coded questions are where the options are specified by the researcher in advance; open questions are where the person being interviewed is free to respond in any way at all. Both have their advantages, depending on the context. The researcher might want to force a choice on some controversial issue; in other circumstances, the researcher might want to find out what the issues are. As always, the design should be chosen in the light of these purposes.

It is generally thought to be a good idea to explicitly offer various kinds of opt-out clauses – no opinion, don't know, none of these, etc. The effect of this is illustrated in an example from a survey in the United States, quoted by Schuman and Presser (1981: 163–9). There were two versions of a question on divorce law:

Version 1: Should divorce in this country be made easier or more difficult to obtain than it is now?

Version 2: Should divorce in this country be made easier to obtain, more difficult to obtain, or stay as it is now?

A randomly chosen half of the sample (760 people) was offered the first version, and the other half was offered the second (770 people). Thus the difference is that the first version did not explicitly offer the option of keeping the divorce laws unchanged; the second did offer this. When that neutral option was given, 40 per cent took it. When it was not given, only 22 per cent volunteered it. Nevertheless, the *ratio* of the proportion replying 'more difficult' to the proportion replying 'easier' was about the same in each case: 45 per cent to 29 per cent in the first version, and 33 per cent to 23 per cent in the second (ratios of 1.55 and 1.43).

Beyond the structure of individual questions, there is also the structure of the questionnaire as a whole. Strictly speaking, we can only discuss this for interview surveys, because there is no easy way of knowing how respondents in postal surveys answer the questionnaire: they certainly need not answer it in the order in which the researcher lays it out. This, in fact, can be thought of as an advantage of interview surveys: you do know what the context of each question was, in the sense of which questions were asked immediately before it. Kalton *et al.* (1978) report an experiment in which the order of the following two questions was varied randomly:

Question 1: Do you think that driving standards generally are lower than they used to be, or higher than they used to be, or about the same?

Question 2: Do you think that driving standards amongst younger drivers are lower than they used to be, or higher than they used to be, or about the same?

The response to Question 2 was the same regardless of whether it came first or second (35 per cent said standards among young drivers were lower). But the response on Question 1 changed according to whether it followed or preceded Question 2. When Question 1 was first, 34 per cent said that general standards were lower; when it was second, only 27 per cent said this. In fact, this difference was due entirely to a difference in respondents who themselves were aged over 45: 38 per cent of them said general standards were lower when Question 1 came first, but only 26 per cent said so when Question 1 came second. Thus, when reminded of the possibility that young drivers might be less competent nowadays (by Question 2 coming first), older drivers were less inclined to rate overall standards as lower.

Given some of the difficulties with getting valid answers from structured questionnaires, researchers have tried to use some compromises between structured and less structured questionnaires. These are sometimes called 'semi-structured', although this covers a great deal of variation in the precise extent of the structuring. Often, in fact, a semi-structured approach is used to test out ideas and wordings before carrying out a larger and more formal survey: thus semi-structured interviews can provide information similar to that of a pilot survey.

For example, Hakim (1987: 30) describes a study of new types of home-working which were emerging in the UK in the mid-1980s (that is, work done in a person's home and paid for by a contractor). Because this was a new phenomenon, the researchers could not have drawn up a standardised questionnaire: they would not have known what to ask about. So interviews were carried out with about fifty home-workers to explore the reasons they undertook home-work, what conditions they experienced, and how a larger and more structured survey could achieve a high response rate from them.

This can also be done even with postal surveys. For example, over nearly two decades until 1991, the Scottish School Leavers' Survey ended its highly structured postal questionnaires (about young people's experience of school and their intentions beyond school) with an opportunity for open-ended comments. The prompt took this kind of form:

> Would you like to tell us more about yourself, in your own words? What have you been doing over the past year? Do you think you have spent your time well? Looking back, do you think you made the right choices at school? Were you able to do all the subjects you wanted to do? Did you get good advice? Do you think the subjects you have studied will help you in the future?

Many respondents wrote substantial amounts in reply. These comments helped to add validity to the statistical analysis of the structured part of the questionnaire (e.g. Bell and Howieson 1988). They were open to analysis in their own right (Gow and McPherson 1980). And they could be used to improve the design of later surveys in the series (Walford 1988: 251–2).

Validity of structured questionnaires

Another way of considering a model such as that in Figure 6.2 is as a way of identifying the sources of error in response. Groves (1989) mentions three: error from the interviewer, error from the respondent and error from the questionnaire. In this chapter we have been looking mainly at the last of these. But we have also considered the training which inter- viewers should receive in order to help them to take full advantage of the strengths of structured questionnaires, and we have looked at ways in which the questionnaire can be designed to reduce the errors that respon- dents might make. We have not exhaustively enumerated the scope for varying the design of questions, but merely illustrated some of the themes and main issues. Designing questionnaires does have scientific elements, but it is also an art, and draws on the experience of many researchers in trying to overcome the problems in order fully to realise the advantages.

Mentioning these other sources of error, however, also reminds us of the limits to what good questionnaire design can achieve. Consider, first, the interviewer effects. The interviewer has an effect, Groves suggests, in four ways, none of which is directly a consequence of the questionnaire itself. One is due to the interview being a structured social interaction (as we discussed in Chapter 5), and so there will be effects of the interviewer's socio-economic status or age or gender or ethnicity. These would relate to stage 4 in the model of response in Figure 6.2. Second, interviewers might administer the questionnaire in different ways – for example, read it out in different ways or go through it in the wrong sequence. The questionnaire can be designed to be as clear as possible (especially if computer-aided interviewing is used), and training can make the interviewer as proficient as possible, but errors cannot be eliminated completely, because inter- viewers are human and are engaged in a human interaction with the respondent. Third, the interviewer could emphasise particular words in different ways, no matter how rigorous the training and the guidelines. Fourth, interviewers could respond to difficulties that the respondent has in different ways, again despite training and guidelines: this 'probing' and 'prompting' has to take place, and attempts can be made to standardise it (an example is in the box at the foot of Figure 6.3). But full standardisa- tion can never be guaranteed.

The second source of error is the respondent, him or herself. The writing about this has come from two branches of psychology – cognitive psychology and social psychology. The example given earlier, from Cannell *et al.* (1981), is mainly from cognitive psychology, about the way in which people recall things. The most important point to take from this literature is that memory is not just a straightforward process of recall but is, in fact, partly a reconstruction of past events. No matter how standard-ised and how apparently scientific the questionnaire is, as soon as the question has been read, things are in the hands of the respondent – steps 1–5 in Figure 6.2. The social psychological contribution has been to point to the social desirability of certain types of behaviour, certain types of response. A sensitive questionnaire can reduce these problems of memory and honesty, but cannot eliminate them.

Apart from these problems with the limited role which the question-naire plays in the entire process of seeking and stimulating responses, there are also problems of validity in the structured questionnaire, even when it is well designed and when it is administered by experienced and competent interviewers. In other words, there are still obstacles to making valid comparisons amongst groups of respondents. All the things that we have been looking at have been attempts to realise the aim of not imposing a conceptual framework on respondents. The ideal is to gather the unmediated views of the respondents, so that comparisons we make amongst them (or amongst groups of them) will truly reflect reality, and not be contaminated by how we did the research.

To finish, there are four problems with this model. The first is that having that goal inevitably restricts what can validly be asked about. It is simply not possible to avoid having a conceptual framework that is part of your research activities. So sometimes all that can be done is to be abso-lutely clear about your conceptual framework, and part of what you have to report is the way in which this might differ from those of the respon-dents. A small example given earlier was that we could not avoid implying a political framework in asking a question about the balance between public and private medicine. But, deeper than that, there is the intrinsic problem with all structured questionnaires that they divide social reality into discrete components and ask about these in a sequential way. The very act of controlling for variations in discussing a social problem may discard some very interesting features about how people talk natu-rally about them. For example, most people probably do not discuss politics in the highly structured way implied by the survey questions in Figure 6.3. The structure there, with respondent's views first, implies that people move from their own views to judge those of the parties. But there is evidence that people's views are partly shaped by the parties themselves (Converse 1964), which would imply that the opinion-forming sequence could be in the reverse order.

Second, when using a structured questionnaire you have always to be aware of the implications of whatever psychological model underlies the responses. Something like the model that we quoted from Cannell *et al.* (1981) seems to underlie most people's suppositions about how people respond to structured questionnaires. Ultimately, it has something to do with stimulus and response, information and retrieval, and so on. It may well be that that is an appropriate model for the kind of information you want. But if it does not seem to be, then you should think about other methods, or think about other methods as well as the structured questionnaire.

Third, there is still an assumption of some distance between the researcher and the interviewer on the one hand, and the respondent on the other, despite the attempt to get the interview or the questionnaire process into the conceptual world of the person being interviewed. The researcher designs a questionnaire which is given to the respondent: it is mostly in one direction, except in the very indirect sense that the researcher (and the research community as a whole) learns from one survey how to improve the design of others. So, if we think of the interview as being a form of social interaction (as in Chapter 5), then the structured questionnaire is a highly artificial version of this. Whereas unstructured interviewing might try to replicate ordinary social discourse (and anthropological method depends on it), a structured questionnaire simply cannot help being out of the ordinary.

But, fourth, this assumption of distance between researcher and interviewee contradicts some of the other assumptions – for example, that the researcher and the person being interviewed share a common conceptual world. All of the discussion of question wording and of clarifying it depends on there being a shared understanding between the two or three parties to this process – researcher, interviewee and interviewer. And it is possible that there might be communities of understanding which do not overlap or which overlap only to some extent, or which – this is the worst case of all – think they overlap but actually do not. That is one reason why there are such things as interviewer effects associated with social class or gender or ethnicity. Eliminating these is not just about sensitivity and tact; the very meaning of some of the processes being described would be changed, depending on the nature of the people present in the discussion. We discussed interviewer effects more fully in Chapter 5. But partly incompatible conceptual worlds are not due only to interviewers. They are probably unavoidable in social research, especially if the researcher is linked in some way with a government agency. We return to this point in Chapter 9: policy research, if it is to be useful to policy makers, cannot help being somewhat distanced from people who do not have power.

None of these four problems fundamentally invalidates structured questionnaires, but they do indicate that we have to think very carefully about where their use is most appropriate and for what kind of information they are best employed. They are particularly useful for factual information, and, even within an opinion survey, factual questions allow us to establish how representative the sample is by comparing the pattern of responses with known characteristics of the population. This opportunity for rigorous assessment of representativeness is probably, in fact, the most important contribution which structured questionnaires can make; it is something of which less structured forms of research design are simply not capable.

But the problems with structured questionnaires also indicate that, even where they are being used appropriately, we have to interpret the responses with care in the light of explicitly acknowledged theories of the social and psychological processes involved in answering the questions. The ideal use of structured questionnaires allows us to undertake highly valid comparisons – in other words, comparisons that control for many of the usual threats to validity. To the extent that the ideal cannot be realised, structured questionnaires at least do have the enormous advantage that they offer structured ways to think about the threats to valid comparisons. The models underlying the use of structured questionnaires may not be valid; but at least they are clear models, offering clear ways of allowing in our analysis for departures from the ideal.

7   Fieldwork

This chapter is about fieldwork and the use of fieldwork in a research design. The term is often used in a more general way than we shall use it later in this chapter, simply to make a distinction between, on the one hand, research which is fairly clearly detached from its context and, on the other, fieldwork – research which takes place in the 'field'. Examples of the former kind of research are archival and library work, mail surveys or experiments in a laboratory setting. Doing library research in one library is intellectually and methodologically like doing it in another. Fieldwork cannot be sharply distinguished from the locale in which it takes place.

There are many very different research designs which involve fieldwork in this sense, employing a broad range of research methods – including observation and interviews, both formal and informal. A researcher, carrying out a series of semi-structured interviews with senior managers in an organisation, might refer to this process as fieldwork; so might another using a much more structured protocol with the same group. Researchers studying a school playground and observing children in that setting over a period of days, weeks or even months would do the same. Survey agencies even refer to the time during which the interviews with a carefully pre-selected sample will be carried out as the 'fieldwork period'.

In this chapter, in contrast, we focus on fieldwork which involves *participating in the everyday life of the 'field'*. Fieldwork, in this general sense of the word, describes the activities that take place in a particular research locale over the medium to long term. It is a process, starting with the task of obtaining access to people and events in an area, organisation or community. The researcher then studies the locale by living or working there for a period of time, or by making repeated visits. Eventually the fieldwork period comes to an end and the process is brought to a close by a planned and carefully managed departure.

For one social science discipline, social anthropology, fieldwork in this sense is almost synonymous with the research process. Ever since the earliest days of the discipline, when the focus was largely on pre-literate peoples, social anthropologists have carried out research by going and living amongst those they wish to study (Malinowski 1922; Mead 1943). Clearly, it would have been virtually impossible to carry out these studies in any other way. The fieldwork method was progressively refined to inform and improve collection of the data, the basic material from which social anthropological theory was created. Fieldwork, then, is central to the training of social anthropologists and built into the epistemology of the discipline. Fieldwork as an activity and social anthropology as a body of knowledge are intimately intertwined. No one intending to do field-work should ignore the methodological writings of social anthropologists or fail to read some of their accounts of being in the field.

On the other hand, social anthropologists should not be seen as having a monopoly on the method, and other social scientists, sociologists in particular, have employed fieldwork. Sociologists, possibly impressed by the results of the fieldwork process among pre-literate peoples in remote places, reasoned that one could carry out fieldwork in one's own society, or one very like it. The underlying motivation for employing fieldwork in research design for some of these researchers was in many ways not dissimilar to that of social anthropologists. They went to live in communities of various kinds which were quite unlike the locales with which they were familiar, but were in the same society. In the process, they adapted the fieldwork process to their situation, their research interests and the problems they encountered. A relatively early example, W. F. Whyte's *Street Corner Society* (1955), and especially the Appendix, in which he gives a 'warts and all' account of his work, remains a classic account.

From observation to participation

A more precise classification helps to make sharper the meaning of field-work as we are going to use it in this chapter. Many years ago it was suggested by Gold (1958) that the roles of researchers carrying out empirical research could be seen as ranging along a continuum, a classification which has now become almost taken for granted in the research literature. Gold's continuum runs from participation at one end through to observation at the other, via two intermediate points: the participant-as-observer and the observer-as-participant.

At the fully participant end, the researcher is part of the situation, and indeed working covertly; others in the situation are not aware that the researcher is there to do research. Participation in this sense involves the whole range of normal human behaviour and, of course, only that. It should be understood that Gold uses the terms 'observation' and 'observer' in rather a specific way. There is no implication that, at this fully partici- pant end of the continuum, the researcher uses *only* data obtained by interaction. Such researchers observe in the same way as any ordinary person does in everyday life. The idea of everyday life is the nub of the matter. Gold is emphasising that nothing in the researcher's behaviour can be allowed to give the impression of being apart from the situation so as to observe it dispassionately. In this fully participant mode, the researcher will have an influence on events which is very similar to anyone else in the same situation.

At the opposite end of the continuum, observation, there is no partici- pation at all. Insofar as such a thing is possible, the researcher does not interact with those observed, nor influence events in any way. It would be naive to imagine that being observed has no effect at all on those observed, but it is well established in practice that after a while people come to ignore an observer, and the researcher will have very little impact on what happens. Occasionally, observation can be carried out in ways which to all intents and purposes have no effect at all on those observed. For instance, it is possible to be an observer in a crowd, to use film which has been obtained so discreetly that those filmed were unaware of it, or even to use one-way screens, often in a semi-laboratory situation. When one-way screens are used, with permission, to observe group behaviour, people appear very quickly to forget that the screen is there. However, observation can, like participation, be carried out covertly. For a social scientist to observe crowds in this way, say at football matches, seems unobjectionable, which is fortunate given the impracticality of informing an entire crowd of one's actions and purposes. In other situations, such behaviour raises ethical issues just as serious as those related to covert participation. For instance, the use of one-way screens in situations where people are unaware that they are being observed would be regarded very widely as unacceptable.

In between the two ends of Gold's continuum, participant and observer, he identified two other roles which the researcher can adopt. The participant-as-observer role is the one where the researcher partici- pates in the day-to-day life of the situation being studied, but it is known that she or he is carrying out research, and there is an element therefore of observing the behaviour without participating in it. In the observer-as- participant role, most of the work is observation but the researcher interacts from time to time with those being observed, perhaps to clarify something. It is important to realise that Gold was positing a *continuum* of research roles. In any research situation at any moment in time the emphasis can be more on participation or more on observation, and the balance can change from time to time.

The idea of the observer-as-participant can be seen in a reflexive way as relevant to social research more generally. Researchers using highly statistical techniques and survey data to investigate issues of public concern may also be participants, in the sense that they may participate in public debate about what is going on in society, and this then interacts with the issues they are researching.

The role of the researcher in the situations which in this chapter we are calling fieldwork is broadly covered by the roles in one half of the continuum – the participant and the participant-as-observer.

Participant or participant-as-observer?

Usually researchers adopt the participant-as-observer role. This may still raise doubts about the extent to which the fieldwork situation genuinely mirrors everyday life; those with whom the researcher lives or interacts are aware that this is not a conventionally straightforward living relation-ship or interaction. This is even more apparent when one considers that fieldwork is often the research design preferred by people studying a social situation which is very unfamiliar to them, or indeed culturally distant from them.

As mentioned earlier, for many Western anthropologists this has been the most frequently encountered situation, although in more recent times some anthropologists have studied sections of their own society. When we do this it raises sharply the question of when, if ever, we are carrying out fieldwork in situations in which issues of cultural distance do not arise. If the researcher works in a situation other than the one in which they grew up or spent a large part of their lives, the sense of being an uninformed outsider arises, whether the research locale is culturally very distant from their previous experience or much closer to home. When Anthony Cohen, as an English anthropologist, carried out his celebrated study of Whalsay in the Shetland Isles (1987), he was on less unfamiliar ground than he would have been among the Kalahari bushpeople, but it is a matter of degree rather than a sharp distinction. A more finely balanced example is Michael Burawoy's study (1979) of an American industrial manufacturing plant. He worked in the plant as a machine operator and adopted the fully participant role. He had the necessary skills to do this and culturally was able to play the role sufficiently well, as is evidenced by the fact that the fieldwork succeeded. In part, this was because the workforce of an urban industrial plant is more heterogeneous than are the inhabitants of Whalsay. Burawoy did not stand out in the same way as Cohen did.

Although one may have reservations, there is ample evidence that fieldwork properly prepared and entered into comes to approximate quite closely life as we know it. Whether a social scientist or not, we 'experience' what is going on in our society, in a sense which is different from our cognitive 'knowledge' of it. It is experiential knowledge which we are trying to access in fieldwork. Certainly, it enables us to access it more directly, more naturally and in a less mediated way than does an interview programme or a survey.

Although Burawoy and others have been able to succeed in the fully participant role, it raises such massive problems of feasibility and ethics as to rule it out entirely in the view of most social scientists. The ethical issue is of course not clear-cut and each researcher must make up their mind on the issue. However, the niceties of ethical judgement often do not arise. Feasibility generally rules out the fully participant role. Even where it might be possible to approach fieldwork in such a way, there are powerful practical arguments against so doing. The costs of failure are extremely high in that those being studied would be unlikely to forgive the deceit if they were to discover that they were being studied without their consent, or spied on, as they might interpret it. Sometimes such an event could involve physical risk; it might also damage the research of other social scientists more generally. Not only are the costs high but the chances of failure are high also. Fieldwork is always somewhat difficult and stressful. Few researchers have the skills to play a role so perfectly over a long period that they give no hint of their 'real' reason for being in the situation. Additionally, a good deal of conventional fieldwork behaviour becomes nigh on impossible. For instance, it is much harder to find opportunities for note taking, some questions which could be asked by a fieldworker known to be a researcher are ruled out, and leaving the field situation from time to time is far more difficult. Crucially, the fieldworker's range of techniques is severely constrained. In the participant-as-observer role, skilled fieldworkers make use of the stranger's licence to ask questions, and they may quite systematically seek information from a number of people, possibly even using an interview approach. We shall in the rest of this chapter discuss fieldwork in the more usual participant-as-observer mode.

Why fieldwork?

We pointed out in the chapter on interviewing that while it is in one sense quite unsurprising that many social scientists tend to think immediately of talking to people when it comes to data collection, this is by no means a universal reaction. Nevertheless it is a common starting point, and not only do many social scientists think of talking to people, they think of one very special form of talking to people – asking them questions. The two previous chapters have been about research designs employing interviews and structured questionnaires. We have stressed that when one asks people questions in an interview situation, it is a particular kind of social encounter with its own interactional rules. It is vital to grasp that this is so whether the interview is of a very structured or virtually unstructured kind, whether one uses a questionnaire or the sketchiest of interview guides, whether one fills in a schedule or tapes the interviews for future transcription, and whether one treats the 'subjects' as respondents or tries to enter into a more reciprocal kind of relationship. People are so familiar with the interview both as a research tool and in their everyday lives that its unusual characteristics, to which we drew attention, go almost unnoticed. These interactional rules of the interview are fundamental to the process. Undoubtedly, the interview has proved itself capable of yielding valid information. As an intrinsic part of a research design, interviews offer a reasonable chance that we can achieve some control along with meaningful comparisons.

In the first chapter of this book on comparison and control we pointed out that comparison is deeply implicated in the normal processes of social life. If this is accepted, we suggested that it is likely that comparison will turn out to be a fundamental part of the research process, because that process is itself part of social life. In a similar way, those social scientists who study the many facets of everyday life, whether in communities, organisations, or larger collectivities such as towns and cities, may sense that there is something slightly strange about the way social scientists so frequently ask questions. After all, the usual interactions of everyday life entail asking questions only in a minority of situations; we do not proceed through our daily routines by the Socratic method, establishing what we know and conveying our meaning to others by a process of question and answer. Furthermore, all who live in society (or most of them anyway) have to be expert everyday analysts of social life, because that is how we make our social lives work.

This suggests that researchers may wish to tap those expert everyday analyses. Studying social life, we can argue, may sometimes be more effectively carried out by research procedures which more closely mirror life itself. If we are all expert everyday analysts of social life, yet we achieve this by living in the situation rather than asking questions about it, can social scientists turn this to their advantage? Many social scientists find it intellectually and personally attractive to adopt the position that the analysis of social life is best carried out by research procedures which more closely resemble everyday social life. This, then, places the emphasis on living in the situation, on observation, on conversation and on casual interaction rather than, say, on the interview, be it formal or informal. As we argued in Chapter 1, comparison and control are part of everyday life. In carrying out fieldwork the researcher both experiences this process in the way that those living in the situation do, and uses the fieldwork experience to form a cognitive understanding also shaped by comparison and a search for control.

Underlying the fieldwork approach, therefore, is the conceptual underpinning that social life is something to be understood through interpretation. From this perspective, the social order is seen as interactive and negotiated, and it is this negotiated social order which we seek to understand and explain. This is what fieldwork is good at. Incorporating fieldwork into a research design is only worthwhile if this negotiated social order and the culture in which it is embedded are at the heart of the research question. The social order can be seen as negotiated and sustained in interactional processes taking place in relatively small groups, and replicated continually and countless times throughout the organisation, association or community. Fieldwork provides the researcher with unparalleled opportunities to access these processes and the meanings associated with them. Arguably it is the only way to do so.

It is for this reason that some social scientists, including many social anthropologists, might argue that fieldwork is the 'only true method' of social research. From such a perspective, fieldwork *is* the research design. It will be chosen almost automatically as the preferred approach, and the problems become questions of the appropriate locale(s) in which to carry it out, the time to be spent in the field, and how to make appropriate comparisons and achieve some degree of control. It should be quite clear from earlier chapters that we would not take this extreme view. For us, the crucial issue is what is gained and lost when fieldwork of this kind is included in a research design of which it may be but a part. There is a sense in which fieldwork is implicitly involved in most research designs, because researchers so often make use of insight and knowledge obtained as a result of living in the society. We shall take this for granted in what follows, and concentrate on fieldwork as a specifically planned component of a design.

Is some fieldwork appropriate in every research design?

As we have said, fieldwork is exceptionally good at providing access to the negotiated social order, and the everyday processes through which it is negotiated and sustained. Some social scientists are so attached to field-work in an almost ideological way that they lose sight of its strengths and weaknesses, and imagine that it is appropriate for everything. Because fieldwork gives access to the details of everyday life, and because researchers gain close, sometimes intimate, acquaintance with those with whom they interact, it is easy to imagine that we should use fieldwork in any research design which is concerned with the more intimate details of social life. Nothing could be further from the truth, and a little reflection shows why this should be so. Because, as we have already said, we are placing emphasis on living in the situation, in observation, in conversation and in casual interaction rather than interview, it follows that it may be exceedingly difficult to obtain access to behaviours, views and interactions which are not normally part of these aspects of everyday life. Such information may be more effectively obtained, for instance, by semi-structured interview. Let us examine this a little more closely.

The researcher in the fieldwork situation will inevitably become well known in the research locale, and will become extremely well acquainted with some people. This is of course a double-edged sword; the more familiar and friendly the researcher becomes with some people, the more others will become cautious or wary, either because they do not entirely trust the researcher to keep confidences, or because their circle of friends and acquaintances does not interact with those of the researcher's closer contacts. Researchers doing fieldwork always have to strike a careful balance, something which is closely connected to achieving a degree of control. There may be a pay-off from a close relationship with someone in the field situation, a special informant, but there will inevitably be costs. Such an informant may be willing to discuss some topics in which the researcher has a keen interest in much more detail and with greater openness than could ever be achieved in an interview. Yet simply reflecting on our own social lives tells us that we might well be prepared to tell an interviewer whom we know we shall only meet once, under strict conditions of confidentiality, things which we do not discuss even with quite close friends in the course of everyday social life. Fieldwork is an essential element of research design where we seek to investigate the interactive and negotiated social order. If the researcher wishes to elevate fieldwork to the status of *the* research approach, then all the research problems they tackle must be accessible to the technique. From our perspective, field-work is no different from other elements of research design.

It is of course possible to combine interview techniques, especially unstructured ones, with fieldwork proper, and indeed this is very frequently done. But fieldwork of the kind we are discussing in this chapter involves observing and recording while participating, generally asking no more questions than any other person in the situation would, and possibly seeking answers even to 'stranger-appropriate' questions from a small number of 'informants'. Strangers are expected to be naive, and the further distant the researcher is seen to be from the culture the more is such naiveté expected and tolerated. Thus, as the researcher's familiarity with the fieldwork situation and those within it becomes greater, the advantages of the 'stranger' role disappear to be replaced by those of the 'insider' role, and the everyday life aspects of the fieldwork approach come into their own. We have repeatedly emphasised in this book that research design is always a matter of compromise. As this process takes place, the advantages of being a stranger, especially a stranger entering a person's life once, never to be seen again, disappear. Obviously, the longer one spends in the field, the more one is expected to 'understand' what is taken for granted by those inside the culture. The more one becomes an everyday participant, the more one is drawn inevitably into groups or activities which may limit access to other groups and activities. In this way, fieldwork can reach a stage of diminishing returns. These diminishing returns can, of course, result not from any real achievement of closure, but from perceptions becoming blunted. It is surprisingly easy in an interview to hear what one wishes to hear or what one believes it is likely one will hear. In the same way, fieldwork can develop a routine quality. The researcher 'knows' what is going on, and that is what they see. This problem is an extreme example of a failure to maintain 'control' in the sense in which we use it in this book.

Comparison and control in fieldwork

Meanings are elicited from the situation by observation, by listening, by interpreting and, of course, by the occasional question, all backed up by introspection. The researcher operates at levels of explicit awareness which we do not use in everyday life, one of the reasons why fieldwork is exhausting. It can be all too engrossing, it may over-absorb us so that, as we relax and over-identify, we cease to be able to observe and analyse and make the appropriate comparisons critically. This is a familiar phenomenon, and many expert fieldworkers have stressed the need to leave the field from time to time, to disengage.

During fieldwork, a cyclical pattern of research is taking place quite different from the linear pattern familiar in some kinds of research. We do not start with some ideas we wish to investigate, gather the data, analyse it and then write it up. We start with some research questions and with some conceptual ideas, to be sure, and we then gather or absorb data, recorded in our field notes, on our tape recorders, or sometimes as visual images, which we constantly analyse and write up, leading to further research questions and a developing conceptual framework. Of course, this conceptual framework as it develops is tested; and the literature is full of devices for doing this, of which searching for the discrepant case and then analysing it is one excellent example. In interpreting the 'data', the researcher constantly asks how good the evidence is for the inference which they are drawing. The data comes from what people say and feel, how they interact with others and what they do in different situations, and these data are constantly cross-checked as fieldwork proceeds. As the researcher develops an understanding of what is going on, or an explanation for something, alternative understandings and explanations are considered, modified, incorporated or cast aside.

It is because the social picture is built up in this painstaking way, because we seek to explain processes, that fieldwork is often said to produce high levels of validity. Control is achieved by these myriad instances of cross-checking, considering alternative explanations, and so on. Whether control can possibly be as effective as in an elaborate experimental design is debatable; certainly it is achieved, if it is achieved, in a very different way.

Unless they are working covertly, researchers living in the situation are neither experiencing quite what others experience, nor relating to others in quite the same way as they do. This creates a tension, wherein lies a danger. Fieldwork can invoke in the researcher a strong emotive attachment. Despite its many strains, it can be very enjoyable. It is attractive because it seems to be more 'natural', closer to life as it is lived. Like many attractions, this can prove fatal to the task in hand. Researchers can easily become so absorbed in the field situation, so engrossed in the business of 'being' rather than researching, that they entirely cease to research, becoming part of that which they set out to study. The researcher always has to maintain some degree of distance and detachment in order to continually evaluate what is going on, fitting it into the analytic frame provided by their professional knowledge and training. Few, perhaps none, of the social situations in which a researcher might wish to do fieldwork are devoid of conflict, tension and competition; social divisions are always present. Undoubtedly, such divisions are more acute in some situations than others. The closer the social scientist is to those involved, the greater the danger of being co-opted by one group or another, and the greater the risk of the researcher losing the confidence of or access to one group because of being perceived as sympathetic to a member of another.

Reactivity is classically seen as a threat to control. Because the fieldworker is participating, it is undeniable that they will have some kind of influence on what happens. At an extreme they may be encouraged by others to be proactive. They may be personally tempted to involve themselves in this way. However, we have already seen that reactivity is an unavoidable element in most research designs. The impact of the researcher on the situation is dependent on many factors. Fieldwork throughout a large organisation, or in a sizeable community, is less likely to change behaviour than is research among a small group of people. Over a long period of time individuals will give various accounts to the fieldworker which can be more effectively cross-checked, compared with and related to what others say, and above all interpreted, than anything that is said in a single interview, be it structured or unstructured. These accounts will inevitably be affected by the relationship which has grown up between the researcher and that individual, because what we say in everyday life to one person we would not say to another. It is again a question of compromise. We have to balance that reactive effect against the control achieved.

How long does fieldwork take?

Fieldwork can only be seen as a cyclical, methodical process in an analytic sense. On the ground it requires the researcher to stand back a little and review what has been happening if the process is to be made visible. One of the problems of using fieldwork in a research design is allocating an appropriate amount of time to it. In principle one would want the process to continue for as long as it takes, and the question is then how long that is likely to be, and how one will know that enough has been done. Although it is impossible to lay down hard and fast rules, what is fairly certain is that large claims are sometimes made for fieldwork which is so brief that the problems outweigh the gains.

Frequently, the answer to the question is determined operationally rather than intellectually. Most research projects are constrained by the amount of money available or, often the same thing, the amount of time. If such constraints are weak, the answer to the question must relate to the aims of the fieldwork.

The researcher may feel that the fieldwork can begin to be brought to a close when they obtain a sense of 'closure', that nothing new is emerging, that fewer and fewer anomalies are being discovered so that the developing conceptual framework is able to handle more and more of what is being encountered. Such a state of affairs can only be reached with regard to a fairly well-articulated set of issues, problems and questions. It is always possible to see ways of extending the scope of a study in order to justify a further spell in the field. Furthermore, the social world is continually changing, albeit generally slowly, so that there will always be more to observe, to participate in and to understand. All research designs should have a beginning, progress through a process, and arrive at an end. This applies especially to fieldwork; the researcher needs to develop criteria by which it can be judged that sufficient time has been spent in the field. The more explicit these criteria, the easier it will be to convince others that this is the case.

Fieldwork reviewed

It is unfortunately the case that, just as cobblers used to recommend using leather, many researchers who are enthusiastic about fieldwork tend to adopt fieldwork techniques as the core of their research design almost automatically. They see it as the appropriate approach to all social science, rather than to some social science. There is, fortunately, an element of self-fulfilling prophecy about this, because it is also the case that the kind of research problems they choose to tackle are indeed those for which fieldwork is appropriate, although we would argue that all researchers could usefully consider incorporating other methods into a design along with fieldwork.

It is probably a less serious matter that there are many people who do not even contemplate using a fieldwork approach as part of their overall research design. The considerable investment required both personally and in time is, reasonably enough, seen as a deterrent. However, giving serious consideration to what might be gained by doing fieldwork can be a useful exercise, focusing the researcher's mind on weaknesses in a design.

A research design may appear intellectually outstanding; the researcher or an outsider assessing it may be convinced that it is as near to perfection as such things ever can be. But this is not enough. The researcher must be convinced and able to convince others that the design is 'do-able' and, crucially, that they are able to do it. Anyone who has, for whatever purpose, assessed research designs put forward by various individuals knows that, astonishing as it may seem, such research designs are sometimes not do-able, or not do-able by the person concerned. It is difficult and time-consuming for researchers to achieve high standards of excellence by using several approaches. Triangulation, though we applaud and recommend it, can be costly.

Serious fieldwork is not only difficult to do well, but it also takes a long time, and for this reason may be difficult to combine with other approaches. In professional research teams this can sometimes be done by a division of labour and members of a team applying their particular skills to a common task. The lone researcher needs to be reasonably sure that they are suited to doing fieldwork and are able to devote sufficient time to it. It should not be undertaken lightly, and should only be incorporated into research designs for which it is appropriate. Fieldwork involves such a heavy commitment that one should always ask whether the same ends might be achieved more easily, cheaply and, sometimes, reliably. The commitment extends beyond the fieldwork period.

The writing up of fieldwork raises complex issues which are beyond the scope of this book. The cyclical nature of the process should ensure that the researcher leaves the field with a well-developed conceptual framework, and frequently is better placed to start writing up than those who have conducted an interview programme. However, properly conducted fieldwork generates a vast amount of data. The normal practice is to write up one's field notes daily, with longer analytic pieces being written from time to time. Checking and rechecking, going over such large quantities of documentary material, is very time-consuming.

Fieldwork is an immensely rewarding activity which deserves a central place in many research designs. It should only be carried out by researchers who realise how difficult it is, prepare adequately for the task and, above all, realise that scholarly interpretations of social life do not spring out at the fieldworker, but are the result of intense and usually lengthy struggle.

8   Time

In the course of this book we have frequently encountered the following problem: because social scientists study a social world which they themselves inhabit, it can be a considerable effort to challenge and confront the taken-for-granted aspects of that social world. Few things exemplify this better than the concept of time.

Time is deeply ingrained in our everyday lives. We use clocks and watches as a matter of course. We take the accuracy of even the cheapest watch for granted, yet in the seventeenth and eighteenth centuries the lives of countless seafarers were lost because of the problems of determining longitude with sufficient accuracy to avoid shipwreck (see the fascinating and accessible account in Sobel (1996)). Devices such as video recorders and answering machines are not just convenient technological developments. They enable us to shift time to our advantage so that we can watch television programmes or answer the telephone when we wish to and not when those designing broadcasting schedules or cold-calling to sell us products think we should. Time provides the common yardstick which makes it possible to catch trains and aircraft, assess the achievements of athletes and complain when we think the referee should have blown the final whistle. There are poems, songs, plays and novels about the passage of time, and innumerable jokes involving time – all an indication that time is deeply significant to the human condition. Yet we seem to experience time in a very simple and familiar way.

It requires a real effort to appreciate how complex the idea of time is, and the ways in which it influences research in the social sciences, and the research designs with which we are concerned. Of all the topics which we discuss in this book, time is both one of the most fascinating and the one for which a single chapter is the least adequate. The relationship of time to the social sciences and thus to research design and the analysis of data is the subject of an ever-growing and, it must be admitted, difficult literature. All we can do in this book is to provoke thought and further learning by pointing out both the need to consider time and how exceptionally complex this can be.

The whole notion of time is not straightforward. There is a sizeable literature on time in philosophy, a literature outwith our detailed professional competence. But there is a useful if contested distinction made in that literature which originates with the Cambridge philosopher John McTaggart (1866–1925). This distinction is between two kinds of time, according to how time is categorised. Events can be categorised at any one moment as belonging to time past, time present or time future. All events can be so categorised, but as time progresses they pass from one of these categories to another. What is now in the present will eventually be in the past; what is now in the future will eventually be in the present and then in the past. Differentiating in this way according to criteria of 'pastness', 'presentness' and 'futureness' is referred to as the 'A' series. But one can also categorise events temporally according to whether they occur before or after each other. Unless we make an error of categorisation, this relationship is invariant; if event '1' occurs before event '2' this will always be so as they both move from future to present to past time. This before/after series is known as the 'B' series. In philosophy, McTaggart started a debate about the reality of time, to which, for him, these two models are central. We are not concerned here with the philosophical debate. For our purposes the distinction is helpful because it illuminates time in social science. We as social agents live in a world in which we experience life as past, present and future. We reminisce about, sometimes learn from, and have beliefs about the past. We experience and sometimes claim to 'live for' the present. We look to, anticipate and try to control the future. The 'A' series is relevant to our social lives and resonates with the way we experience them. But we also build up temporal maps of our social world which depend on the sequence of events, regardless of whether they are in the past, the present or the future. Regardless of the standpoint from which we view these events, conception occurs before birth, marriage before divorce, the birth of our first child before that of our second, and the whole of our lives before death. Time is a powerful tool in research design and data analysis precisely because of this 'B' series notion. This is causal time.

Time impacts on social research in two conflicting ways. The study of economic, political and social processes is a central task of social science, and we have already seen that some research designs and the methods embedded in them offer more direct access to process than others. One of the attractions of observing over time, or doing fieldwork over time, is that it can give the researcher a firmer grasp of process, always providing that the length of time involved is sufficient for the process to develop or make itself visible. Thus a research design involving fieldwork which is based on too short a fieldwork period may well be more misleading than illuminating. Because many research designs only obtain a snapshot, they lay themselves open to serious errors if they attempt to make inferences which are, explicitly or implicitly, time dependent. Some research designs only give us access to the present, and one-shot cross-sectional surveys for instance, as is clear from earlier discussion, have to be treated very cautiously. Obtaining survey information relating to several time points gives us a firmer grip on process. We can then use the idea of time positively by tracing events through time.

But, if we recall yet again the central theme of this book, that the crucial issues of research design are comparison and control, nothing makes these, especially the first, quite so difficult to achieve as the existence and passage of time. Time poses problems as well as yielding vital information on process.

The problems illustrated

A fairly accessible way into the problem is to reflect a little on the consequences of ignoring time, or perhaps more precisely the meaning of time. A very common way of studying social life is to identify members of a sample who have certain life-events in common. We might for instance carry out research on a group of people who have experienced something or have some characteristic. Consider first such a study looking at people who have experienced the death of a parent. Few researchers, even those embarking on research for the first time, would do this without enquiring into the point in the life-course when the death occurred; that is, when those people we are considering acquired the characteristic in question, that of having experienced the loss of a parent. It is obvious that the age at which this occurred may be absolutely crucial. The death of a parent in one's older years is to be expected; such an event in childhood is another matter entirely. We can respond to this in several ways when designing the study. We might decide that our particular interests should lead us to concentrate on a sample of young children who have lost a parent. Even here, intuition, the literature or our ongoing research might suggest that we should make finer divisions within the childhood period; never to have known one's father may have different implications than losing one's father at the age of 5 years old. Such a design, focusing on young children, would be appropriate if we are interested in the impact of the loss over a relatively short period – perhaps in a study of immediate grief. It would be impossible to make reliable inferences from this about the longer-term effects over time of losing a parent in childhood. Here we require a quite different design which compares, at differing points in the life-course, people known to have lost a parent in childhood, perhaps at appropriately chosen different ages.

All this is fairly self-evident. Few researchers would fail to reason in this sort of way. In other cases it is less obvious unless you train yourself always to look for the impact of time. Thus, we might study the unemployed, and if we were not familiar with the literature, treat them as a single group. But only a little reflection shows that we need to classify them by age because, as in the example above, we can see at once that being unemployed at 50 years old is different from that experience at 25 years old. Again, the point in the life-course when the event occurred may be critical. Not much more sophistication is needed to see that being unemployed for a month is different from being unemployed for two years. Thus how long the event persists in the life-course enters the picture. Comparing the two events, bereavement and unemployment, we can see that some life-events, such as birth, death, leaving school, voting in an election or the birth of a child, occur at a moment in time, although their impact may persist. Other kinds of event, such as unemployment, have a start point and an end point at a moment in time, but themselves are associated with the passage of time: one is unemployed for a period of time. We may wish to compare people who have experienced a long period of unemployment with those who were unemployed for a shorter time. It is less immediately obvious that being unemployed for a month as opposed to two years is a different experience for a 25-year-old and a 50-year-old. Thus both the duration of the event and its onset are of importance, because the 25-year-old and the 50-year-old person have traversed a different life-course and are at different points in the life-cycle, with different memories of the past and expectations of the future. Of course, this period of unemployment might be the first in their life or the latest in a long sequence of such periods, and yet another variable enters the analysis. Much less immediately apparent is that the age at which they *first* experienced unemployment is suggested by some research to be crucial.

Thus, in considering a study of the impact and meaning of unemployment, we have thought through a series of different time-related variables. When did the event occur in the life-course? How long did the event persist? Does this second variable have a different impact according to when the event occurred in the life-course? For those of a statistical turn of mind, we can assess the effects of a variable measuring the age at which the event occurred (t_1), and a variable measuring the length of time over which it persisted (t_2). But we cannot leave the analysis there because there may be a statistical interaction between t_1 and t_2. Next we have the number of times the person has been unemployed and further complexity.

On the face of it, having many spells of unemployment might seem more serious than being unemployed once. Yet being unemployed ten times for a week may have very different consequences from being unemployed once for two years. And finally we have the variable measuring when in the life-course the person was first unemployed. Depending on the exact focus of our study, some or all of these time-related factors may have to be taken into account in our research design.

Cohorts and cohort studies

A good way to start thinking about the research design issues is to think about one's own life-course. First, there is something one shares with everyone who was born on the same day in the year. We are not here referring to the obvious, that is that one shares a birthday, although it might conceivably be of interest. For instance, people born on Christmas Day, or 1 April, or perhaps a leap year day, might have more in common than those born on most other days in the year. More relevant for our purposes, however, is that these people born on a particular day are the same chronological age, and up to a point this is something which affects their behaviour, beliefs, and so on. We refer to people of the same chrono-logical age as an 'age cohort'.

There are several important and well-known longitudinal studies of samples of people who were born on the same day or in the same week in Britain. They provide data gathered at various points in the lives of these people, and although they are extremely expensive to carry out and main-tain, they are among the most important sets of survey data available in Britain. The National Child Development Study (NCDS), for instance, in 1991 completed its fifth wave as they are called; that is, the fifth time the entire sample (or as much of it as can be traced) has been interviewed. This produced both a cross-sectional set of data about a sample of a particular age (33) and also, when combined with the previous waves, a longitudinal data set. The research design is thus of repeated studies of the same sample of people born on a single day or in a single week in a partic-ular year. The length of time which is allowed to lapse between waves is an intrinsic part of the design.

In this latest wave of the NCDS, data has also been collected on the children of the panel, and it is worth considering just what conclusions we might extract from these data, because doing so begins to alert us to the kind of problems which arise. If you have a random sample drawn from all the people born on a particular day in a particular year, or indeed the entire population of people born that day, it is clear that as the study progresses through time the data represent information about the life-course of people born at that point, to which the life-courses of those born, say, five years before or after that date are likely to at least bear a strong resemblance. But their children present an interesting set of conundrums. Certainly they are the children of the original sample or population and we can say a lot from that. They tell us about the children born to a group who themselves were born on a particular day in the past, whose life-courses, as we have just seen, are likely to represent perhaps a decade of people. We can learn a great deal about generational change and the transmission of advantage and disadvantage, be it physical or social. But the data on the children are not representative of anything else and one has to be very careful when making comparisons. For example, those children born to the cohort who are now aged 5 years old, say, are not representative of 5-year-olds generally in Britain because they are unique in one crucial way. They are 5-year-olds, one of whose parents is precisely a particular age. And given patterns of assortative mating, most of the couples are roughly the same age. If, on the other hand, we took a random sample of 5-year-olds, their parents would have widely differing ages between, shall we say, 22 and 55 years old.

Age effects, cohort or period effects, and individual effects

The discussion thus far has introduced in a general way some of the underlying ideas involved in analysis of data over time. We now turn to presenting these ideas in a somewhat more formal way.

We have the idea of the age cohort as a group of people of exactly the same age. In practice we would nearly always use a rather broader brush and work with a cohort of people born in the same year or group of years. Thus when analysing data obtained from a sample of people we might divide them into age bands – cohorts – aged 20–29, 30–39, 40–49, and so on. In this way one can reduce a mass of data to manageable proportions, and in most studies, where sample size is limited, obtain sufficient numbers in the various categories to be meaningful.

If we compare two different cohorts not at a moment in time but when they are both the same age, say between 40 and 50 years old, there will be broad similarities. Simply as a result of chronological age the people in the two cohorts will change in similar ways and will resemble each other at particular ages. We frequently analyse data by age, essentially comparing different cohorts one with another. The underlying assumption is that, for our purposes, differences *within* the cohort will be less important than differences *between* them. People aged 20–29 will differ from people aged 30–39 or 50–59, and these differences will be greater than those within the age group. The process is made more complicated by the fact that age is not just a matter of the passage of time but has a social meaning. Thus, while all those aged 50–59, say, will have certain attitudes and patterns of social relations in common, the subjective meaning of age differs in different social groups. For all that, however, analysis of data by age, the comparison of different age bands with each other, does often yield significant patterns, and for now we shall take that as given: getting older has social consequences.

The question we now have to ask is this: are the differences we observe between the age groups really the result of ageing and ageing alone? This is by no means a safe conclusion, as we shall show later when we discuss age and Conservative voting. As we have already mentioned, those people born in, say, a particular decade will up to a point have broadly similar life-courses. The life-courses of our hypothetical cohorts are affected by much more than the ageing process itself. Suppose we did a study way back in 1995. Consider first the members of the cohort who were, say, 60 years old at that time. They were affected by the consequences of living to be 60 to be sure, but they have also lived not through a random sixty years but a particular sixty years, those from 1935 to 1995. If we are carrying out our study in Britain, this means they experienced the Second World War between the ages of 4 and 10 years old.

We might have been comparing this group with the group who were 70 years old in 1995 and been tempted to attribute the differences we saw to the ten-year age difference between the groups – to the ageing process. This might be anything but a safe conclusion. This group who were 70 years old in 1995 were born in 1925 and would have experienced the Second World War between the ages of 14 and 20 years old, and it is easy to see how different an experience that was. Just to make the point even more forcibly, consider the group aged 50 in 1995. They were born at the very end of the Second World War and were young children in the years of austerity which followed. Being a particular age then has consequences which are a product both of getting older, and the events which occurred during the life-course as a person was a particular age. Suppose we compare the 50-year-olds with the 70-year-olds in the above example. The former would have learned of the Second World War from their parents, might have been brought up by a person who lost their partner in the War, and were exposed to a diet which some people believe was healthier than that experienced by the 30-year-olds in our study who were born in 1965. The 70-year-olds, born in 1925, would have been old enough to have experienced the War as adolescents and adults, possibly even to have served in the armed forces. The differences between these various cohorts would be due not just to their stage in the ageing process.

What we are talking about here is referred to as the difference between an 'age effect' and a 'cohort effect'. The difference is easily seen in an oversimplified example. Wendell Wilkie, a Republican candidate for the Presidency of the United States, famously remarked that 'any man who is not something of a socialist before he is forty has no heart; any man who is a socialist after he is forty has no head'. If we observe in a general sample that older persons are more inclined to vote Conservative, two possible sharply contrasting inferences are open to us: that as people get older, they become more Conservative – an ageing effect; or that these people have *always* voted in that way, with those born earlier more inclined to vote Conservative, those born later less inclined, and will continue to do so – a cohort effect. It is immediately apparent that these two inferences would have dramatically different consequences for the Conservative party. The first inference suggests that the pool of Conservative voters is constantly being renewed, the second that it is being steadily diminished unless an entirely new cohort starts voting for the party.

As we mentioned briefly earlier, we do not have to make our comparisons solely between age groups, comparing for instance those aged 30–39 with those aged 40–49. We can, given adequate sample sizes, cut the cake another way and compare two cohorts when they reach the same age. Thus we can compare the people who were born in 1925 with those born in 1935 when each group reaches the age of 60, or enters the age group 50–59. Here we are comparing two cohorts when they are the same age rather than two cohorts at the same period in time. In principle, if you have sizeable samples and you compare these two cohorts born in 1925 and 1935 at the age of 60, you can tease out something of the impact of the events of the period they lived through. You can separate the age effect and the cohort effect.

If we wish to do this, the impact on research design in our hypothetical example is easily seen. Ideally, we need to access data obtained in studies carried out in 1985, when the first cohort was 60 years old, and in 1995 when the second cohort reached that age. This means either carrying out an over-time study, or carrying out a study in 1995 and obtaining highly comparable archive data relating to 1985. Less ideally, we could have carried out the study in 1995 and asked respondents for data relating to 1985. The problem here is that obtaining information about events in the past depends heavily on the accuracy of recall, and the process of recall is prone to error. People forget things and make a guess, or simply cannot provide the information. Events are recalled in the light of subsequent experiences and the past is frequently rewritten, because either it presents the person in a more attractive light, or makes them appear more knowledgeable, prescient or in tune with the times. A classic and simple example is the tendency in post-election studies to find more people who claim to have voted for the successful party than is indicated by the ballot results, and indeed more people who claim to have voted at all than was the case. We discussed these 'recall effects' in Chapter 6.

Time impacts on events and life-courses in these two different ways: it impacts in a general way, where its passage brings with it inevitable changes; and it also impacts in a more specific way, where events and processes occurring at certain moments in time impinge on different ages and groups of people differently. We have thus far thought of cohort changes as resulting from fairly time-specific events such as the Second World War. There are, however, rather longer-term secular changes occurring over a period of time, sometimes referred to as 'period effects', which have to be considered as potential cohort effects along with more precisely time-bounded events. To separate these two kinds of cohort effect is generally extremely difficult and often impossible, but this kind of change has always to be kept in mind. Thus the widespread application of the computer or the computer chip in practically every area of social life has had a dramatic impact on everyone in the last twenty years. These general secular changes have in some ways impacted differently on different cohorts, and in other ways affected the population more evenly. The way in which the effects are interwoven can be seen clearly if we compare two groups of 60-year-old persons, one today and the other only a decade ago in 1990. The latter would have had almost no acquaintance with computers; the former would have some, even though both these groups would have had less acquaintance than contemporaneous 20-year-olds.

In focusing on age and cohort effects we have thus far downplayed individual effects. Of course, these are a constant concern of social science. When we analyse data statically, at one moment in time, using cross-sectional data, we constantly compare one grouping with another based on independent variables at the individual level, measured at a particular moment in time. Examples might be the comparison of men and women, different social classes, or groups with different levels of education.

When carrying out over-time or life-course analysis we are then faced with the extremely difficult problem of disentangling age, cohort and individual effects. One of the things which makes it problematic is that the effects 'interact', as statisticians would put it. To revert to our original example, being 60 years old in 1995 will impact on one's health. Coming from middle-class rather than working-class origins will also affect this. But growing up between the ages of 4 and 10 years old during the Second World War, as this cohort did, might have had a different impact on middle-class kids than on working-class kids. The individual attribute of class alters the way the cohort effect impacts. Similarly, some events, such as a major war or an important change in legislation like an Education Act, do affect all members of a cohort; other events will only affect some members of a cohort. The collapse of the mining industry might be an example here.

Time and different research designs

Research designs which enable us to tease out these various effects with any certainty, and at the same time cope with the usual problems of random variation, are seldom achievable, especially in small-scale research. Even with very large amounts of survey data of a valid and reliable kind, and high levels of measurement, the statistical models required are highly sophisticated, and even disputed amongst researchers with high levels of statistical and mathematical competence. This should not deter novice researchers of a quantitative turn of mind and appropriate interests from carrying out secondary analysis on such large data sets, after appropriate training and with adequate support, but the difficulties have to be appreciated.

All researchers, however, need an adequate understanding of the relevant concepts. We cannot stress too strongly that no person embarking on research can afford to ignore the impact of time and the challenges it brings with it. It is not acceptable to assume that the analysis of time-dependent data can safely be left to one's highly quantitatively inclined colleagues. An understanding of the general principles underlying the analysis of time-dependent processes is extremely important, if only to alert the novice researcher to both the pitfalls they bring and the leverage which obtaining data over time provides. As a rule of thumb it is almost always true that a design which allows one to take account of time, in one way or another, is better than one which does not. Researchers who are alert to the tricks which time can play with inferences are better equipped than those who are not. The topic is most easily presented in a rather formal way, as we have just done, but time plays a part, whether or not explicitly recognised, in much social scientific research, whether it uses quantitative data sets, qualitative material or both.

Our message to the reader, then, is that the proper study of society insists on a time dimension although handling this dimension is a constant challenge. Throughout this chapter we have sought to illustrate how different research approaches and designs tackle the issue. We conclude by summarising these designs more programmatically. We would not go as far as arguing that we should simply give up cross-sectional studies, snapshots at one moment in time. This is too extreme and would be to preclude a great deal of valuable research. But it is as well to be aware of the dangers. Techniques are constantly being improved and developed which liberate us partially from the appalling risks of drawing certain kinds of conclusion from cross-sectional data. The next step is to have repeated measurements at different times.

Three types of quantitative survey-based approach

First we have the more quantitative, survey-based approaches. We need to distinguish between *cohort studies*, *panel studies* and comparisons of *repeated cross-sectional studies*.

We have already touched on cohort studies. The best-known existing studies have taken all the births in a particular area on a particular day or in a particular week and then followed the sample for as long as funding is available, intellectual curiosity persists and human tenacity prevails. Just to keep in touch with the sample and persuade them to be interviewed or provide data in other ways at regular intervals is an enormous and highly specialised undertaking. The tyro researcher, and indeed most experienced researchers, can only use such a research design by tapping in to existing cohort studies. There is no intrinsic reason why the study has to commence at birth, and a cohort could be picked up at any age by suitable sampling techniques and then followed over time. If we are interested, say, in the years between the ages of 50 and 80 in order to study the onset and period of retirement, then it is not very efficient to start with a birth cohort and wait fifty years to start work. Even if we pick up the cohort at age 50, the study is going to take a long time to bear full fruit. We shall return to this in a moment. However, as we have repeatedly emphasised, nothing is perfect in research design. If we do start the study at age 50, the automatic downside of this is that any information obtained about the first fifty years of the life-course will be retrospective.

In a panel study, a sample is taken from the population at a particular time and those people are then followed up and re-studied at regular intervals. Crucially, the members of the group will not all be the same age. The rationale behind panel studies tends to be different from that for cohorts. The emphasis in a cohort study is generally on the life-course, on people's demographic behaviour, health or economic activity over a lifetime. The interest is in explaining how the lives of different groups unfold as they get older. As a result, interviewing is generally carried out with fairly long intervals between waves. The respondents in the fifth wave of the National Child Development Survey were 33 years old. In panel studies, re-interviewing tends to be much more frequent. The British Household Panel Study interviews annually. In the major panel studies the sample is generally representative of the whole population, or, say, the whole adult population, although it is entirely possible to design panel studies of highly specific groups (see for instance Fraser *et al.* (1998), which describes the career progression of a sample of teachers). For researchers with limited resources this may be a viable and effective option.

The emphasis in panel studies is on change at the individual level or the household level, and on how change impacts on different groups. When the first findings of the British Household Panel Study emerged (Buck *et al.* 1994), the research team rightly emphasised how it showed a much greater amount of change in the course of a year than was usually assumed. For example, between the fourth quarter 1992 and the fourth quarter 1993, more than a quarter of the population experienced a substantial change in income, equally divided between income falls and rises (83, 91). Only two-thirds of panel members placed themselves in the same financial management category, where the researchers used a frequently used way of classifying the way couples organise their finances (220, 230); the cross-sectional distributions, however, are virtually identical (228). A research design using a panel, even over as short a period as a year, may then enable us to tell a very different story from a cross-sectional study.

Social scientists have known for decades that apparent stability can conceal enormous change. A well-known example comes from voting studies (Lazarsfeld *et al.* 1948). If one studies intended voting behaviour in the run-up to an election, the overall percentages opting for the various parties at two different times may remain quite stable, leading one to infer that voter preferences are settled and little change is taking place. If one obtains these data from a panel one may find that this inference is entirely unjustified. One tends to find that the relatively fixed marginals conceal large numbers of individuals changing their intended vote but in such a way that intended vote losses for the various parties are balanced by vote gains. A more recent example comes from a study of the closing stages of the 1987 election campaign. A panel was interviewed four times, in March, mid-May, late May and mid-June. Of those who responded in all four waves, only 63 per cent remained faithful to the same party throughout (32 per cent were Conservative supporters, 17 per cent Labour and 12 per cent Alliance). A remarkable 38 per cent of the electorate changed their declared voting intention one or more times in the space of three months, from one party to another or between a party preference and being undecided. In the first fortnight of the campaign, the Tory vote remained stable at 44 per cent, but they lost 5 per cent and gained 5 per cent (i.e. about a quarter of the Tory vote). Similar figures can be shown for Labour and Alliance. In the last week, the Tory vote apparently declined from 41 per cent to 38 per cent, but this involved losing 6 per cent and gaining 3 per cent, again a shift of around a quarter of their final vote. The Alliance vote in the final fortnight remained apparently stable at 24 per cent, but this concealed losses of 8 per cent and gains of 8 per cent, a total of two-thirds of their vote (Miller *et al.* 1990: 234–5).

We come now to the third of these different research designs. In repeated cross-sectional studies we compare samples studied at different times, but consisting of different people. For all the reasons just outlined, these studies are excellent at allowing us to assess structural changes and the impact of events intervening between survey waves, but one has to be very cautious about making inferences concerning individual change. Techniques for analysing data sets of these kinds have been greatly developed in recent years; there are many statistical problems which are not immediately and intuitively obvious.

One of the biggest and best-known regular cross-sectional surveys is the decennial Census. The Census provides a nice illustration of the different design issues. For most of this century the Census has been a series of cross-sectional studies of the entire population, a 100 per cent sample with data available only at a high level of aggregation and not at the individual level. It is compiled primarily for governmental administrative use but is used widely by social scientists because, although the data collected are limited, the sample is huge, and the data are collected and coded to a very high standard. Studies based on data from more than one Census are, then, a prime example of the use of repeated cross-sectional samples. In the 1970s, pressure, mainly from social scientists, led to the creation in England and Wales of a longitudinal data set whereby data in the 1971 Census for a sample from the total Census were linked to the data for the same individuals in 1981, and subsequently in 1991 (see Hattersley and Creeser 1995). This has so far created a three-wave panel study with unusually large intervals between the waves. Various other forms of demographic data have also been linked to this data set which can be used by social scientists generally, although in order to preserve confidentiality there are tight restrictions on the analysis which is permitted. Finally, as mentioned in Chapter 5, in 1993 a cross-sectional data set with data on 1.1 million individuals and 276,000 households was extracted from the 1991 Census for England and Wales and made available. Similar data for Northern Ireland was made available in 1994. These data sets allow for much more refined analysis of the cross-sectional data than in a normal survey. When similar samples of anonymised records are available from the 2001 Census, over-time comparisons of the two cross-sectional studies will be possible.

There is one further topic we wish to discuss in this section. As we stated earlier, it is possible in a cross-sectional design to obtain some of the advantages of a panel, if one collects retrospective data and is prepared to confront the problems of collection and recall which this presents. It is feasible to collect data which covers a surprisingly long time span, and thus combines some of the strengths of both the cohort and the panel study designs. In particular, researchers have collected data in cross-sectional surveys describing in considerable detail the respondent's work and life history. In this way it is possible to place an emphasis on aspects of the life-course usually only tapped in cohort studies. The sample is across most of the age range, and some of the restrictions of the cohort are avoided at the cost of having far fewer respondents in any one age band.

Because the technique in this design depends so heavily on the quality of recall, a great deal of attention has to be paid to the detail of data collection, and the type of material which can be covered is limited. It is probable that very few people remember with any great accuracy how they felt about things or what their attitudes were thirty, twenty or even ten years ago, though hard evidence one way or the other is limited. Even strictly factual information may be misremembered or perhaps distorted by the effects of time. The ESRC's Social Change and Economic Life Initiative collected detailed life and work histories by using grids with time along one axis, expressed both in terms of the year and the respondent's age in that year, and the types of information along the other axis. These grids were filled in by the interviewer in a collaborative exercise with the respondent, and seeing the events of their life laid out in front of them was both intriguing for the respondents and seemed to act as an *aide mémoire*. Events which came earlier came physically earlier on the grid; one might think of it as time in the sense of both the 'A' and the 'B' series with which we started this chapter. As the focus was on a particular year, events were recalled from the standpoint of that time as being in the past, the present or the future; viewed as a whole the events lay before the respondent in a before/after pattern. The study built on experience gained some years earlier in the analysis of data from the National Training Survey 1987, and especially the subsequent collection and analysis of an extensive work history in the first systematic examination of women's work histories (Elias and Main 1982; Martin and Roberts 1984). Gathering these histories generates enormous quantities of data and analysis is complex, but, with careful cross-checking, high levels of control can be achieved, and powerful comparisons made between different trajectories through the work history or the life-course.

Life histories

Instead of collecting a life history in this way, another research design of a more qualitative kind is the life history as collected over a period of time by repeated interview. If this less structured approach is to pay dividends, it is essential that the depth of data obtained compensates for the loss of control. The sample size is generally small, the information sought much more personal and the description much 'thicker'. Social scientists using this research design recognise that one has continually to bear in mind that what one is hearing is an account of the past as seen from the present. The date of one's first marriage is usually likely to be reported in a survey with a fair degree of accuracy by both parties. The bride's or bride-groom's feelings on her or his wedding day as reported twenty years later will inevitably be refracted through the experiences they have had since then, and in particular those relating to the marriage. Comparison of their accounts, and those of their lives since the wedding day, together with much cross-checking in the course of a series of interviews, may enable us to infer cautiously what they might have said at the time had they been asked. This, together with the accounts they give seen from the stand-point of the present, can be compared with those of other couples to great effect. Much oral history is of this kind, and some memorable studies have been done (e.g. the examples given in Dunaway and Baum (1997)). The samples may be very small indeed – an account of one person's life at the limit (see the examples cited in Chapter 4).

The life history had a vogue in sociology's past, especially as associated with the Chicago school, and produced some classic works. It is perhaps no coincidence that one of the first people to use and write about the life history approach was Dollard, who was trained originally as a psychiatrist. In Chapter 5 we mentioned the monumental work *The Polish Peasant in Europe and America*, written by W. I. Thomas and Florian Znaniecki (1958), and based on letters written by the subjects – accounts describing their lives. Thomas and Znaniecki claimed that 'personal life records, as complete as possible, constitute the *perfect* type of sociological material' (quoted by Graham Bowker (1993)). Graham Bowker was writing on the revival of the life history, which gave rise to some outstanding studies from the Chicago school of sociology in the 1930s, subsequently virtually disappeared in social science, and has enjoyed new popularity in the last twenty years (for a summary see Smith (1994)).

Modern approaches to the qualitative life history, however, do differ considerably from the earlier ones. As we hinted above, there is now less interest in whether there is a 'true life' which can be recovered if you get the method right, and more in the life history as a retrospective reconstruction of the past, not necessarily distorted malevolently out of a wish to mislead but subject to memory lapse, to selection, to constant rethinking and re-assessing. The emphasis of this particular research design is then on comparing the ways in which people construct and reconstruct their lives, and how biographical information is used in the interactions of everyday life.

Social science as history and time as a topic in its own right

We wish in conclusion to this chapter to brush lightly over two points. First, let us recall what we wrote earlier about the historical nature of social science. There is a real sense in which 99 per cent of social science is history, very recent history. We nearly always study the past, although in doing fieldwork we do manage to get to study the present some of the time. But by the time we write it up, it is the past! There are some nice questions about how much more difficult things get as we go further back in the past, but many of the issues of evidence are the same. Associated and even more intriguing questions concern the circumstances under which and the extent to which we need to understand the past in order to interpret the present. Here research design and conceptual argument encounter each other. It is possible to offer fascinating and very convincing explanations of much of what we find in the present with no reference whatever to the past, except perhaps the very recent past. The designs we have discussed in this chapter are unlikely to appeal to those who approach their discipline in this way. The more the conceptual emphasis is on process and change over time, the more the researcher has to contemplate using one of these designs.

We conclude this chapter by returning to the fact that time is a topic of study in its own right, and once one starts to think about that, one realises that the whole thing is even more slippery than we have admitted. Time is itself socially created, even in its astronomical or atomic sense, but that is to go far deeper than we intend. Our point here is that time and its passage is *experienced* differently by each of us, and that this is an exceptionally easy thing to understand and intuit but also exceptionally hard to build into one's work. The impact and role of the passage of time on social life cannot be assumed to be constant across social groups, and we have seen that we can indeed take this into account with the right approach and data. But the very meaning of time differs and probably changes over time.

9 Policy research

Research that has some relevance to public policy is a very important strand in social research generally. Policy institutions provide a source of research funding, policy is an influential way in which social science knowledge is translated into social action, and policy making is itself an interesting topic of social scientific study. This chapter considers the nature of policy research and the extent to which it may raise distinctive questions of design. Is studying the institutions of public power any different from studying any other social organisation? Is the kind of research that is useful to policy makers any different from social research in general? Should social researchers be concerned with making their work relevant to policy at all? Broadly, our answer to these questions is that policy research is not a category all on its own: it draws on the full range of social science design. Nevertheless, what researchers (or their sponsors) can do with the results of policy research is distinctive.

This chapter is in three main parts:

- The first deals with the context of research on public policy – the relationship between policy research and the policy process.
- The second deals with epistemological questions – the extent to which the knowledge that is relevant to policy is distinctive.
- In the third, we suggest that there are unavoidable conflicts between research and social policy. They are unavoidable because policy does need to draw on social science, even though a truly independent social science will always be critical of policy.

The chapter concludes with an outline of how the concepts of comparison and control can help to illuminate the discussion of public policy.

A particular form of policy research is evaluation, which Bulmer (1986b: 155) defines as follows:

its aim is to discover whether a particular policy is actively accomplishing what it set out to accomplish.

This would exclude, for example, prospective (or predictive) research, or research designed to examine the relationship among various policies, or research which looked at any aspect of policy that was not part of the original, explicit intention of policy makers. Most of the points we make in this chapter apply equally to evaluation as to more general policy research.

We deal almost entirely with public policy, in the sense of policy which is decided by public authorities such as central or local government, their agencies, and the social partners whom they recruit in pursuing their goals (for example, by contracting out part of governmental activities). We do not deal explicitly with policy issues in, say, commercial companies, although many of the principles we discuss here would be relevant there as well.

Research and policy

If there is a consensus in the academic literature on policy research, it is that the official model of its relation to policy – which is probably also the popular model – is inadequate.

What we mean by the official model of policy making in this debate is summarised by Bulmer (1986c: 5–6) as consisting of five steps:

1   A problem requiring action is identified, and the relevant values, goals and objectives are enumerated.
2   All important strategies for solving it are set out.
3   The important consequences which would follow from these are predicted.
4   The consequences of each strategy are then compared to the values, goals and objectives set out in step 1.
5   A policy is chosen in which the consequences most closely match the values, goals and objectives.

According to this model, social science knowledge can contribute to steps 2, 3 and 4, although not really to the essentially political or moral issues which arise in 1 and 5. Rein and Schon (1977: 235) describe this as the 'problem solving' approach to the use of research to inform policy making. Weiss (1977b: 13) suggests that a refinement of the model could allow some research contribution to the setting of the problem, if knowledge created through research can stimulate policy makers into taking action. But the main role for research according to this model is still in working out the most feasible means towards desired ends.

Bulmer and others have pointed to six ways in which policy making is rarely as clear as the model would imply. These ways overlap and interact with each other, because the real world of policy making does not fit neatly into any categories of theoretical analysis.

The most obvious is that policy is made by the pluralist bargaining of interest groups (Jordan and Richardson 1987; McLennan 1995). Weiss (1977b: 13) describes the resulting knowledge as 'iterative' – not the rational analysis supposed in step 3 in the model above, but a much more diffuse process. Examples abound from public policy over many decades. For instance, the reform of higher education in the UK which started roughly in the late 1980s, and is still continuing, was not the simple outcome of one policy goal followed by research that would evaluate the various routes to that goal. It was driven by numerous influences, such as demographic change, the growing number of young people passing school examinations, the belief that a more highly skilled workforce would make the economy more competitive internationally, and rising educational aspirations. To each of these social changes there corresponded large volumes of social research: indeed, with the partial exception of the trend in examination attainment (on which figures are published routinely), the changes would not have been noticed had it not been for research. Some of that research was summarised in the report of the Dearing Committee in 1997, but the report itself was the outcome of diverse political influences (Neave 1998; Trow 1998). Further research is needed to translate its policy recommendations into practice.

The second of Bulmer's points is that, partly as a result of this pluralism, policy making proceeds incrementally (Lindblom 1980; Hogwood and Gunn 1984; Sabatier 1986). Policy makers do not identify problems in the deliberate way envisaged in step 1 of the official model. Problems arise because they are, as it were, the next thing on the list, often in fact because they have been thrown up by the solution to a previous one. Another way of putting this is that policy development continues throughout implementation. For example, the need to reform higher education was a consequence partly of deliberate changes to school examinations in the middle years of secondary school (the General Certificate of Secondary Education in England, Wales and Northern Ireland; Standard Grade in Scotland). Each subsidiary step in the current reform of higher education raises new policy and therefore research issues in subsequent steps. For example, the decision by the UK Labour government in 1997 to introduce tuition fees, and to replace the student grant with loans, occasioned a new policy concern with preventing this from narrowing access to higher education. These concerns, in turn, required research on whether the new fees and loans would indeed have an impact on access.

Third, the bargaining which leads to incremental change is affected as much by power and interests as by dispassionate science. Weiss (1986: 36–7) argues that research then becomes ammunition for fighting political battles. No piece of social research is conclusive, and so research findings are used selectively by whatever side of the debate finds them most congenial. These debates happen sometimes because the available social science is not very good, sometimes because the research questions which have been addressed by social scientists are not those in which the policy makers are interested, but mostly because important social issues rarely admit of easy resolution. An example would be the debate about academic selection in primary and secondary schools, where the research has such complex results that both proponents and opponents of greater selection can find support in it for their positions (Gamoran 1992; Hallam and Toutounji 1996; Harlen and Malcolm 1997; Oakes *et al.* 1992; Scottish Office 1996). Much of the research on this is rigorous, but that has not prevented the political debates from continuing.

The fourth point is that policy relies as much on what Lindblom and Cohen (1979) call ordinary knowledge as on research (see also Wainwright 1994). Policy makers derive their ideas from common sense, from unsystematic observation, and from thoughtful speculation. As Lindblom (1988: 224) puts it:

> for some complex decisions, rules of thumb and other arbitrariness are, at least on a priori grounds, no less desirable than attempts at rational analysis that cannot be conclusive or even approach conclusiveness.

There are influences from the ideas of politicians, civil servants, journalists, pressure-group leaders, business people, and so on. Bulmer (1986c: 25) points out that the social policy of the post-war and 1960s Labour governments in the UK was influenced as much by the close social contacts between Labour politicians and academic researchers as by rational planning. Some researchers have called this part of the 'assumptive world' of the policy makers: the taken-for-granted knowledge about how policy works rather than the outcome of research conducted and debated rationally. Of course, some of this ordinary knowledge is based on thoroughly rational analysis, and some is even influenced by research. But it is not all like that.

As a result, fifth, the greatest impact which research can make on the policy process is through stimulating what Weiss (1977b; 1982; 1986) calls 'enlightenment'. If policy makers rely on common sense, then researchers have to aim to shape that. As she puts it, 'the ideas derived from research provide organising perspectives that help people make sense of experience' (1982: 303). Concepts probably matter more here than specific empirical findings (Wagenaar *et al.* 1982: 8; Booth 1988). An example would be the ways in which research on poverty in the 1950s and 1960s established that the welfare state had not eradicated it (Abel-Smith and Townsend 1965; Timmins 1996). This public rediscovery of poverty became the common sense of policy makers, and indeed of most people, and was probably influential on the election of the Labour government in 1964. Conversely, when the political climate is unfavourable, even well-conducted research will have little impact. This happened to the Black Report on the connection between ill-health and poverty in the UK. It was commissioned by the Labour government in 1977, but by the time it was published in 1982 the Conservatives were in power and they mostly ignored it (Townsend and Davidson 1988).

Of course, sixth, it is not only the policy elites' common sense that can be illuminated by research. Rational enquiry is part of the whole intellectual enterprise of society. The rational model, in fact, has to come back in here, because it still commands great normative power, being 'a "dignified" myth' (Gordon *et al.* 1977: 29). But it is then only one of several ways of talking about research. Others include the demystifying role of social science, and the capacity of research to set problems, whatever it may do to help solve them. This is an important part of what we meant at the beginning of this chapter, when we said that social science always has a critical role in relation to policy. One important consequence is that research on social policy should be set in a wider study of politics and culture as a whole. Thus, understanding why the old common sense of the 1950s and earlier about intelligence and educational selection was replaced by new ways of understanding children's learning has to pay attention to general changes in society and culture, as well as to specific research on the workings of the selective system. For example, we could cite research which showed that the selective system of secondary schooling in Britain was unfair (Douglas 1964; Floud *et al.* 1956; Glass 1954), but this research on its own would not be enough to explain why a perception of unfairness became so politically potent (Giddens 1991; Inglehart 1990). To understand that, we would have to look to more general accounts of social and cultural change, by which equal rights to social citizenship came, in principle, to be widely accepted.

The character of policy research

Having considered the political context in which policy research is carried out, we now look inward to what policy researchers do. A starting point for discussion is the five features of policy research which Hakim (1987: 3) identifies as being distinctive compared to social research in general, what she calls 'theoretical research'. These are:

- Differences of principle: policy research aims to produce knowledge for action, whereas theoretical research produces knowledge for understanding.
- Contingent differences: that is, differences which, as a matter of fact, tend to distinguish policy research from theoretical research.
- The role of explanation and cause: these matter less in policy research than in theoretical research.
- The types of findings which the two sorts of research produce.
- The inescapably political character of policy research.

This framework from Hakim offers many insights into the character of policy research, and so we discuss it more fully here. But we also have reservations about it, to which we return in the next section.

Action and understanding

Hakim argues that theoretical social research could be characterised by three features:

- It is interested in causal processes and explanations: for example, it would want to discover what the causes of poverty might be.
- The variables it uses are theoretical constructs, in the sense that they have to be translated by the researcher into usable measures. For example, concepts such as social structure or gender are not immediately measurable. They have to be mapped onto observable characteristics, for example people's occupations or people's biological sex. The mapping is itself problematic, insofar as it attenuates the full richness of the theory. Thus gender is a much more complex social phenomenon than sex.
- Its audience is, generally, other social scientists, often in fact the members of just one academic discipline.

Policy research, by contrast, is not particularly interested in any of these things, and is primarily concerned with social action. Thus, although it is not uninterested in explanations, it is often more taken up with description and prediction. For example, policy research on poverty might start with a map of poverty and how it affects people, and then might assess trends creating more or less poverty. Insofar as policy research is interested in explanation, it is only in respect of variables that can be acted upon, because only these are amenable to change by policy makers. Thus governments can do almost nothing to change the class structure of occupations, and so, as an explanation of poverty, social structure is not very helpful to policy. But an explanation in terms of, say, the lack of vocational qualifications held by unemployed people, or the lack of affordable childcare for lone parents, is far more politically useful, because, in principle, these are precisely the kinds of things which policy can affect.

Policy research has an audience far beyond academics, and is almost always multi-disciplinary in any case. Thus a useful characterisation of poverty would draw on sociology, economics, psychology, ecology, and many other types of research. Policy research also has to be persuasive to these diverse audiences; in particular, its results have to be readily generalisable to the social groups served by the policy process which commissioned the research. A piece of policy research into poverty would have to persuade government that its recommendations could be relevant nationally. Otherwise, there would be only a limited amount which government could do to deal with the general problem.

Contingent differences

Hakim argues further that policy research tends to treat respondents as holders of roles, rather than as individuals. For example, they are employers, trade union officials, leaders of pressure groups, or whatever. This is because policy research works in a world that is structured by the immediate demands of policy making. For the same reasons, policy research has to work to a strict timetable which has been set by the policy makers who have commissioned it, and has to make recommendations for action. There is simply not the luxury which purely academic research offers of continually revising conclusions, or of finding the world to be so complex that straightforward recommendations are impossible.

The role of explanation and causation

According to Hakim, a particularly important contingent difference between policy research and general academic research is the role which they each give to explanation. She suggests that theoretical research tends to be mainly interested in the causes (or explanations) of a particular type of behaviour. For example, research into criminal behaviour might look at explanations in terms of socio-economic conditions, social psychology, the media, and so on. Policy research, by contrast, is more interested in the multiple consequences of particular policy innovations. For example, research on numerous training schemes for school leavers in the UK in the late 1970s and the 1980s investigated the many effects which they might have – on employment, on skills, on attitudes to work, on returning to education (Finn 1987; Raffe 1987). Because the causes in question here – the policy innovations – are often at a macro level, the consequences are likely to be very diffuse. The clearest example would be changes in government macro-economic policy, which would have very disparate effects indeed. For example, the long-term effects of the decision by the new Labour government in 1997 to transfer control of interest rates to the Monetary Policy Committee of the Bank of England will take many years to be felt fully, and so evaluating the change will take even longer.

The resulting complexity can make clear conclusions difficult to arrive at. On the other hand, government does have the authority to set up experiments more readily than do isolated social researchers. As a result, policy research can have access to much stronger internal validity than other types of social research. Several examples are discussed in Chapter 2. We return to this issue of the social authority of government later.

The nature of the findings

Hakim suggests that, whereas theoretical research is interested in *whether* there is an association between variables, policy research wants to quantify any association and judge whether it matters in substantive terms. A good example is in research on gender differences in mathematics attainment at school (Kelly 1987; Walden and Walkerdine 1985). It is of great theoretical interest whether there are any stable differences between girls and boys. But, from the point of view of educational policy, what matters is whether the difference is educationally important. Because samples in this kind of research tend to have large numbers of males and females to study, even small differences can show up as statistically significant, even though they might be quite trivial educationally. Small, stable differences might be interesting theoretically in this case if, for example, they corresponded to psychological theory about how men and women learn. But if an average difference is small, then – given the variation in attainment among men and women separately – there will be many men and many women at each level of attainment. So, for policy purposes (such as predicting pass rates in examinations or rates of progression to successive stages of education), the dominant point will be the extensive overlap rather than the small average difference.

Debate

Policy research is unavoidably controversial, if only because people notice it, but also because many vested interests are involved in sponsoring it or in resenting that some other interest sponsored it. This is similar to the point we made earlier when discussing the context for policy research, but it is relevant epistemologically because it clarifies the question of what counts as research. Research is, by definition, confined to studying the past: even research that claims to make forecasts has in fact to rely on extrapolating from what has already happened. This statement of the obvious highlights the boundary to the claims which research can make. As research, it cannot settle what is to be done with its results (the fifth point in the rational model of research summarised above). When the results of policy research are published, they enter the realm of politics and ideology. The researchers can, of course, then join the debate, but they do so as citizens, not as researchers.

Controversies

It is in precisely this area of the controversy generated by policy research that Hakim's account does break down somewhat. Undoubtedly, her analysis has many strengths, and does help us to see some of the things which make policy research distinctive. But, despite the clarity which a sharp distinction between policy research and theoretical research can provide, it is ultimately not tenable in that simple form. Policy research, at some level, ought to address theoretical issues, mainly because policies have to be based on valid social science if they are to work. Most notably, it is all very well saying that policy research need not be so interested in causal explanations as theoretical research might be. In the short term, perhaps policy does not have to know much about why it has its effects. But in the long term, it does have to develop such an understanding even for political reasons, because policy makers have to know how to make the short-term policy permanent, or – if it fails – why it should not be made permanent. An example is in the field of educational research on the effects of school class size on children's attainment. The academic research on this is remarkable for finding very little effect, and yet policy makers and educational interest groups continue to favour a reduction in class sizes (Blatchford and Martin 1998; Blatchford and Mortimore 1994). In the UK, this was one of the main promises which the Labour Party made when it came to power in 1997, and, in the short term, it will measure progress by simply recording whether and to what extent the average size of school classes has fallen. But, in the long term, it will matter a great deal whether or not the academic scepticism about this policy is correct. The aim of the policy is to raise pupils' attainment. If the academics are right, it will fail, and so government will have to explain why. Even if the policy succeeds in raising attainment, the explanation of why that happened despite all the academic research will have to draw on the insights which that research has provided.

More generally, there are two ways in which Hakim's model fails adequately to describe policy research. The first is that it implies that policy research ought to take its problems from government. Of course government is an important source of problems (especially because it would not fund research which did not address its problems), but that cannot be the only consideration for researchers if Carol Weiss's notion of enlightenment is indeed a purpose of policy research. For example, during the 1980s and 1990s, many governments decided that they wanted to evaluate schools by various statistical measurements, and academics in several countries worked out schemes for doing this efficiently (Willms 1992; Reynolds *et al.* 1996). But other researchers have also distanced themselves from government by continuing to ask: why evaluate schools at all? Their argument is not just the moral one that some people – teachers and parents – were questioning the policy. It is also that the policy will not work unless the people responsible for implementing it share the government's perceptions of what the problems are. In short, policy research should not only be about working out the best means to given ends (although this is undoubtedly an important aspect of it). It can also be about questioning these ends, or at least about investigating the extent to which the ends are shared by public-sector professionals, by interest groups, and by the wider society.

The second problem with Hakim's model is a more general version of the first. It is that it incompletely represents the understandings of the subjects of the research. If the problems are defined by government, then the ways in which the research is designed and analysed can distort the relationship between citizens and government. This is not only that the problems which the government wants investigated might not be widely shared. It is, more fundamentally, that the situation might not even be described in the same terms. For example, Brown and McIntyre (1993) investigated what school teachers saw as their daily concerns in the class-room. It turned out not to be what was top of the government's agenda (matters of attainment, for example), but to be about maintaining a normal state of orderly activity. Of course, that state of order might have as its ultimate goal the raising of attainment, but attainment was not the primary focus. Therefore, a full understanding of what teachers do in the classroom would not be possible without taking these perceptions into account. This second problem is exacerbated if the research is conducted by using standardised questionnaires. As we noted in Chapter 6, incorporating the outlook of respondents into the design of these is not easy, especially in contrast to more fluid types of interviewing where the framework of questioning can be modified in response to what the interviewee is saying.

Effective policy researchers have to attempt to deal with these theoretical issues. One model which has been followed is that of 'collaborative research'. According to this, policy research is a partnership between government, researchers and users of the research. This should extend to the choice of problems, the framing of the questions to be asked of respondents, the choice of method (standardised questionnaire or some other technique), the analysis of the data, and the dissemination of the results. There are not many examples of this working successfully, for reasons we come to shortly, but one is the programme of research on students' experience of secondary schooling which was conducted between 1971 and 1991 by the Centre for Educational Sociology at Edinburgh University (Burnhill *et al.* 1987). The essence of the programme was a two-yearly postal questionnaire survey of school leavers, asking them about their experience of school and of the transition to work or further study; further discussion of the methods can be found in Chapter 6. The main funder of the survey was the Scottish Office, a government department, although further sources were other government departments, local authorities, UK research councils and charitable foundations. The design and analysis was a partnership between the academics and the funders, but the condition of funding always allowed the academics freedom to publish anything at all a short time after each survey had been completed. In the late 1970s, further funding from the UK Social Science Research Council allowed this partnership to extend to many other users, through a series of summer schools and a regular newsletter in which people (mainly teachers) could learn how to use the data, could try out research ideas which had arisen in their own professional practice, and could suggest topics for inclusion in later surveys.

Natural questions about such a programme are: why should government cede this amount of control, and why should academic researchers not proceed independently of government? The answer to the first question would mainly be that government needs good-quality advice, and that a good way of getting it is to contract out its work to an independent agency. Independent advice is strengthened if it pays attention to the users of public services as well as to the originators of public policies. In ↘ democracy, it is probably also useful for government to show that it is paying attention to independent voices, and (more cynically) to be able to distance itself from their conclusions if what they are saying is unattractive.

The answer to the question for academics is that, if you are interested in policy research at all, then presumably part of what you want to do is to influence government. Working in partnership is a more effective way of doing this than relying solely on the general social enlightenment which (earlier) we quoted Weiss as saying was the main impact of research. More profoundly, as Burnhill *et al.* (1987) argue, only legitimate government has the authority to command access to regular samples of a population, and working in partnership with such an authority can strengthen the validity of what we do.

But these answers to the questions still assume a degree of common interest between government and researcher. From the government side, it requires a respect for pluralism. For researchers, it requires that the government is politically legitimate: that is, that the government's purposes are sufficiently close to those of the society as a whole that researchers working for government are also, in effect, working for society. Otherwise, researchers who are serving government are not serving society. Apart from the moral dilemmas this creates, it also causes practical problems: for example, what incentive is there for people to respond to questionnaires that seem to come from a governmental system they distrust?

An example from research on Scottish vocational education illustrates the complexity of the problems. The Technical and Vocational Education Initiative (TVEI) was a UK government programme in the mid-1980s which aimed to encourage the technological and vocational education of school and college students; we have already mentioned some of its design features in Chapter 2 (Bell *et al.* 1989; Gleeson 1987; Paterson 1993). In Scotland, the TVEI was very diverse in its implementation, for two reasons, one political and the other social scientific. The political source of diversity came from the controversy with which the scheme was surrounded. In Scotland, it was seen by teachers and others as a threat to comprehensive education, and as a threat to the autonomy of Scottish educational policy making (because the TVEI was initially directed from Sheffield, not Edinburgh). Lying behind these fears was the wider political tension in Scotland between a Conservative government which could command only about a quarter of the popular vote, and a civil society that was firmly left of centre. In response to this distrust, the government ceded a great deal of local control to schools and colleges, which then developed their own projects in distinctive ways. This diversity then also satisfied the scientific requirement that an educational experiment should have a great deal of internal variation in order to be a true experiment (or, strictly, a quasi-experiment: see Chapter 2). The TVEI was officially experimental, and so had to allow the individual projects to try out different things.

In other words, the practicability as well as the scientific validity of the whole exercise required that the government surrender control. The research problem was then whether this necessary pluralism might threaten any attempt at generalisable evaluation. At the extreme, what scope would there be for evaluation if each school or college not only devised its own version of the initiative, but also devised its own rules for evaluating the initiative? For example, what if one school decided to reject all the official criteria of evaluation, such as examination pass rates, interest in industrial careers, and staying-on rates in full-time education beyond school? Could an experiment sponsored by government tolerate that degree of diversity? In other words, could a politically and scientifically acceptable experiment allow methodological pluralism as well as pluralism of materials and approaches?

There are no straightforward answers to these questions, but they do indicate that policy research requires some shared understandings amongst government, researchers and society – here, concerning the purpose of schooling, the importance of vocational education, and the relative importance of the various things which students might gain from education. In the absence of that common world, research would become very difficult. But so would government itself. So the conditions for feasible policy research are actually quite similar to the conditions for the feasibility of any legitimate government at all.

As a postscript to this story about political pluralism and research pluralism, the intensifying conflict between the research community and the Conservative government came to a head in 1992 when the Scottish Office withdrew the funding for the two-yearly surveys of school leavers that had been conducted by the Centre for Educational Sociology (CES). Although never officially admitted, part of the reason was almost certainly that the CES had repeatedly come into conflict with the government over its research findings (*The Higher*, 14 February 1992: 7). Both sides would claim that the other was politically motivated, but this simply illustrates the point we quoted from Carol Weiss earlier – that because the findings of social research are rarely conclusive, there is scope for research to be used by all sides in political conflicts. For government to sponsor research that might be used by its political opponents is, in one sense, more than can reasonably be expected. But it is also the necessary condition of pluralistic research that contributes to a genuinely common social endeavour.

Comparison and control

None of the discussion in this chapter shows that policy research is methodologically distinctive in any systematic way. It might tend to rely on statistical surveys more than ethnography, and might not tend to use exploratory methods, but it does not differ in principle from any of the approaches we have looked at elsewhere in this book. Like them, it therefore depends strongly on comparison and control. Nevertheless, it does use distinctive combinations of methods, and the relevance of comparison and control is undoubtedly conditioned by the policy context.

Comparison is crucial, because most policy research depends on comparing some policy options with others. This is another way of stating the inadequacy of the official model of policy making and research (which we outlined at the beginning of this chapter). Good policy research acknowledges that the policy agenda always contains more than the government admits. The other ideas come from the pluralism of policy making, from ordinary knowledge (including the knowledge required during implementation), and – in a democracy – from popular views about what policy should do. Government may not like it, but all these conflicting views and experiences have to be analysed if we are to form an adequate judgement on how any particular area of policy is working. Good government depends on recognising this, even though it may restrict the scope for government action. And independent research is essential if government is to gain a truly plural picture of what its policies are doing.

Research control, on the other hand, is very difficult. Usually governments want results quickly, and only rarely are they willing to sanction the complexity of a proper social experiment, although they sometimes are. In any case, even governments cannot ensure complete control of conditions: this is another consequence of the pluralistic processes which influence policy making and implementation. From the point of view of government, what works is more important than what is scientifically valid, and making things work is as much a matter of political bargaining as of scientific design.

10 Journalism and literature

In this final chapter, we discuss forms of evidence that are not conventionally thought of as social scientific. We concentrate on print journalism and novels, but similar things could be said about broadcast media, video, film, drama, song, poetry, and so on. The rationale for doing this is summarised by Glaser and Strauss (1967: 162–3), although they were writing only about sociology. Sociologists, they say, have focused too much on verifying theory, and insufficiently on generating it. 'Documentary materials', they say, 'are as potentially valuable for generating theory as our observations and interviews.'

There are three ways in which these might be useful for investigating society:

- The first is where the thing being studied, for example a newspaper, is an object of study for what it reveals about society.
- The second is as a source of straightforward information about society.
- And the third is the most distinctive: these writers are treated as commentators as well as recorders.

The three approaches are not wholly distinct: they overlap, as we shall see.

Before we come to these three, however, it is worth drawing a distinction from a fourth way in which a newspaper or publisher could be studied. They could be interesting because they are simply important social organisations. For example, the sociologist Tom Burns developed some influential views on the nature of bureaucracies and hierarchies through research on the BBC (Burns 1977). Although the fact that it was a broadcasting organisation could not be ignored in such research, the primary interest was in the way it was organised rather than in what it did. A similar point could be made about Cynthia Cockburn's study of print workers in the British press (Cockburn 1983). Her primary focus was on the meaning of skill and its interaction with gender and social class. These interesting studies are not the kind of topic we deal with in this chapter. For our purposes here, what makes a newspaper, say, different from other social institutions is that its main business is itself analogous to research: it, too, seeks to understand other social phenomena.

As objects of study

The first approach to this area of research would ask what the content of a newspaper tells us about wider social development. Three examples can illustrate this.

The first is the book by Alvar Ellegård called *Darwin and the General Reader* (1958). It traces, in great detail, how the thinking about natural selection and the theory of evolution entered into the popular press after the second half of the nineteenth century. Ellegård was using periodicals as an index or as a window – as a way of seeing how society was thinking.

A second example is a study by H. F. Moorhouse of the changing perception of Scotland v. England football matches between the late 1960s and the mid-1980s (Moorhouse 1989). He traces how newspapers regarded hooliganism. In the early years, he found widespread disapproval in both the Scottish and the English press. By the mid-1980s, when the government of Margaret Thatcher was in power, and when Scottish voting preferences were becoming increasingly anti-Conservative, even the broadsheet Scottish newspapers such as the *Scotsman* and the *Glasgow Herald* were saying that hooliganism was unfortunate but an inevitable outcome of these political tensions. The English press, by contrast, remained disapproving.

A third example comes from the historian William Donaldson (1986). He studied the popular press which emerged in Victorian Scotland after the repeal of the Stamp Act in 1855 and the consequent fall in the price of publishing. He used his study to seek to understand the relative importance of the weekly press and of the book trade in shaping popular culture. He found that the press dealt with serious contemporary matters. His conclusion was that 'the popular press played a major role in a communications revolution of lasting significance for contemporary Scottish culture' (1986: xii). As with the other examples, Donaldson was treating the press as a source of evidence about society's self-consciousness.

Something very similar can be done for literature, and indeed Donaldson deals with serialised fiction as part of his more general study. A sustained and now influential study of novels from that point of view is provided by Lukács (*The Historical Novel*, published in 1962). He was interested in the emergence of the historical novel, with writers such as Walter Scott, and its development into one of the ways in which European and North American societies tried to understand themselves in the ensuing 150 years. We return to this example later.

The model, then, that underlies this use of the press or of literature is, first, that they have a wide readership and therefore are important. Strictly speaking, of course, it should be incumbent on the researcher to actually demonstrate that they have a wide impact as well as a wide readership. It is much easier to show that newspapers are bought than that they are influential, but in an open market, over a long period of time, journals with high circulation are presumably influential, at least on the terms of debate. Donaldson, for example, could produce evidence that readers did respond to what the popular press was offering. Easier to demonstrate is that newspapers or novels are influential on key people, because they cite them in their own writing or speaking.

Now, the difference from the Tom Burns and Cynthia Cockburn examples is that we are treating the media as special kinds of cultural products explicitly concerned with the circulation of ideas. This use of the media and other means of communication is similar to the way that historians and sociologists have used other social institutions concerned with circulating ideas – for example, churches or political parties. Emmanuel Le Roy Ladurie's account of the village of Montaillou in the South of France was based on that village's remarkably good historical records (Le Roy Ladurie 1978). They existed because it was one of the centres of the Catharist heresy in the early fourteenth century and, therefore, attracted the close attention of the Inquisition. Ladurie's account reads very much like a novel. The detail of the historical record is such that he can attempt to recreate the personalities of the individuals involved. He is particularly interested in the way in which the dissenting church acted as a circulator of ideas. For example, one particular shepherd followed an annual migration across the Pyrenees between Provence and Catalonia, following pasture for his flock. He took back and forward with him his Catharist beliefs. So part of Ladurie's interest is in the interaction between the material circumstances of this man's life and his role in spreading new religious ideas.

Our purpose, then, in this first use of the media, novels, and so on, is in studying them as things that are concerned with the circulation of ideas. Of course, one of the things we then find is that some of these ideas are themselves originally academic ideas, because researchers contribute to the media and journalists quote their results. But the primary focus is not on academics, but on the many more other writers who write about social life. So the main questions for research design are the same as in any other use of documents – how do we select material from the media that is representative?

As sources of information

The second and third approaches to documentary material that we deal with are different from the first one in one important respect: they both treat the journalist or the novelist as a colleague, not as an object of study. Of course, the distinction is not as stark as that. Journalists writing about Scotland v. England football matches are both involved in the events and also commentators on them. Researchers can study them as participants (our first approach) and enlist them as allies (our second or third). The distinction is blurred further when researchers themselves sometimes become the object of media attention, which may bring into question their objectivity or their claims to understanding. Educational research in the UK has been subjected frequently to this kind of scrutiny. The distinction is worth making all the same, even if it has to be a matter of roles rather than people. As researchers, we should be clear when we are adopting the outlook of the journalist or whomever (the approaches we are turning to now), or analysing that outlook itself (the first approach dealt with above).

The second approach is where newspapers, for example, are used as factual records. Thus newspapers, television, novels, plays and poems can be used as sources of information. In some ways this seems a very natural thing for us as social scientists to do. But, of course, we have to be convinced of the reliability of what purport to be facts. For example, it is now standard practice in academic political science to use newspapers as records of elections. There is a series of books published to coincide with every British general election since 1945, and they not only study the media's influence on the campaigning but also use the media as a main source of evidence (for example, Butler and Kavanagh 1997). This use of the media is based on the idea that the journalist has access to a particular type of fact or a particular view of what the facts are which is not shared either by the participants or by academics. Some types of academic journal contain contributions from journalists for this same reason, for example *Parliamentary Affairs* and *Political Quarterly*. It has been suggested that this closeness of academics to journalists is especially notable in small countries where there are fewer of each than in large ones (McCrone *et al.* 1989). Thus there are frequent contributions by journalists to periodicals such as *The Wales Yearbook* and *Scottish Affairs*.

A similar point can be made about novels. The novels of Charles Dickens are a source of information about social conditions in nineteenth-century England. The novels of Upton Sinclair or John Steinbeck provide similar sources for the Depression years in the United States. It is not accidental that these authors were critics of the social status quo. That is why they were compiling the facts about what was going on. Their political orientation should, of course, make us cautious about how reliable they were, but no moreso than about campaigning journalists or statements by government agencies. That they might be only partially reliable does not mean that they are wholly useless. In some sense, they – like the social scientist – are providing accounts of social processes.

This use of fictional forms to record something about society is very common indeed in the popular media. Some of the most widely watched television programmes are not just fiction. In fact, they presumably have their big impact precisely because they are also partly true. In the UK, television drama series such as *Brookside* deal with domestic violence and drugs, and the series *Casualty* generated controversy because it appeared to be critical of Conservative government policy on the health service. A famous example from the 1960s is the television drama *Cathy Come Home*. It led to the setting up of the organisation Shelter which campaigns on behalf of homeless people; in many ways, the programme actually created 'homelessness' as a social category. So studying popular fiction can give us some kind of insight into what is going on in society.

In some senses, the truth or otherwise of what is being portrayed matters less than the fact that it is widely perceived to be true. For example, in one controversial episode of *Casualty* in 1994, a woman died because a hospital casualty department had been closed down and she could not get to the one remaining open in time. For social research, it does not matter much whether or not that was an accurate picture of the effects of government policy. What really matters is that this was watched by about eight million people. It then becomes a political fact that a very widely watched television programme was representing the effects of government policy in a particular way. If we did not pay attention to that, we would be missing something about the social world of the people we are studying. If you only did questionnaires or even in-depth interviewing, and ignored this programme, you would not get a full picture of how people felt about the state of the health service. So the partiality of these novels or dramas is itself interesting.

The model here is of the media or of novelists as recording devices and, in that sense, as no different in principle from questionnaires or interviews or some other method. Indeed, the media itself uses these other research devices. So the journalist or the writer is, in that sense, our research collaborator, in somewhat the same way as an interviewer in a survey is our collaborator. The journalist or novelist might also help to set an agenda. For example, Upton Sinclair's novel *The Jungle* about the animal slaughterhouses in Chicago helped to instigate legislation to regulate that trade.

The great advantage of using published documents or filmed material in this way is accessibility. Newspapers are very accessible, unlike, for example, historical records, and it is easy to go back for more. You can go and study a newspaper and take some information from it and you always know that you can go back to that newspaper and get more information. (Unfortunately, television and radio programmes are, if anything, less accessible than historical records.)

What you cannot do anything about – and this is the principal disadvantage – is that these writers might not have asked their questions in the ways that we would have done. So using journalism or literature is like doing secondary analysis but with the extra problem that we do not know what the writer's research design was. The concept of research design is not, on the whole, relevant, although something analogous to it is. A serious journalist will attempt to gather evidence systematically; a thorough novelist will do research into the subjects of the novel.

Moreover, the selection bias with this type of information is different from the selection bias that exists in historical records. One of the problems with historical records is that the ones that survive tend to be the ones that have been sponsored by the winners, the powers that emerge from some conflict. Historians are trained to ask 'In whose interest was it that this document should have survived?'. With journalism or literature the problem is not quite like that. Questions of power do, of course, arise, but they do not prevent the powerless from appearing in novels to a much greater extent than in official documents, as the example of Dickens illustrates. But that example also shows that the bias arises because the novelist's or the journalist's facts have usually been selected as part of an argument, even if the argument is only to provide an account. Dickens, indeed, uses the power of the facts to persuade us that the people about whom he is writing are real, and then their reality in turn makes the facts more persuasive. Dickens was also a campaigning journalist and essayist. He started the journal *Household Words* in 1850 to proclaim his opinions on pressing social matters. As a journalist, he did quite a lot of observation and fieldwork walking around London. He even wrote quasi-journalistic accounts of his travels in America and in Europe, especially Italy.

Similarly, and more recently, the journalist and poet James Fenton, writing about his experience of reporting the war in Vietnam, says that all he wanted to do was to provide an account of what was going on: 'journalism becomes unnatural when it strays too far from…reporting' (1988: xiv). But, in deciding what to report, he had to persuade himself first of all what the truth was that he wanted to convey. That truth, in his view, was that what was going on was not what was being put across by the public relations agencies of the US government. Although he would say that he was presenting the facts against the ideology of the American government, nevertheless, behind these facts, there was a decision as to what was true.

So, with novels and journalism, there is no visible research design which enables us to judge whether the comparisons made are driven by some convincing conceptual or theoretical starting point, nor whether the writer has employed a method which gives us reasonable confidence that they have ruled out competing explanations on grounds other than not liking them. But this is emphatically not to argue that we cannot treat journalists and novelists as fellow social scientists in the sense that their insights, information and analyses are frequently more penetrating, enlightening and infinitely better written than the more pedestrian efforts of 'real' social scientists. It is more a question of asking what additional evidence, or data, or fieldwork, or information about the way the material was obtained one would need to have before citing the analysis in the same way as a journal article. After all, many journal articles are open to exactly the same criticism, and we would not cite them unchecked or unsupported.

As privileged observers

This apparent problem of selection bias brings us to the third and the most distinctive use of journalism, novels, and so on. This is where we do not treat these people just as colleagues; we treat them as privileged observers, as having a way of viewing society that we do not have, at least in our capacity as social scientists. In this case, the selection bias is the way in which novelists or journalists sacrifice some generalisability in exchange for much greater validity than social research can usually achieve. They make their accounts authentic.

This is the most difficult use of these forms of communication, but it is also that which makes greatest use of their special characteristics. The reason for the difficulty is that – as many literary critics have pointed out – the truth of literature does not necessarily depend on its factual accuracy or in its research design, or in anything that we might recognise as social scientists. The same could be said for journalism.

To illustrate this, we look first at some extracts from Tolstoy's novel *War and Peace*, in the translation by Rosemary Edmonds (Tolstoy 1957). (The idea for using this example comes from Lukács (1962), who expands on it further.) The novel is enormous: about 1,500 pages in most editions. The last forty pages, however, are not what you would expect. They are an essay, of exactly the same kind as Tolstoy's more political or academic contemporaries were writing – people like Marx, Comte and Mill. It is a

straightforwardly social scientific essay on the nature of free will in relation to historical events, 'in what way individual persons made nations act
in accordance with their will, and by what the will of these individuals
themselves was controlled' (Tolstoy 1957: 1275). So it is the familiar sociological problem of structure and agency. However, Tolstoy obviously did
not believe that his preceding 1,450 pages could have been reduced to the
forty pages of essay, and the argument he would use, like most novelists,
would be that the purpose of the 1,450 pages is to give us access to what a
social scientist would call validity. The bald account, in terms of structure
and agency, cannot do that, and therefore we can treat the main body of
the novel as a vast qualitative study. The force of these 1,450 pages lies in
what the literary critic would call aesthetic persuasiveness; not facts, not
description, not theoretical analysis as in the essay at the end, but something to do with the aesthetic qualities of the writing. That is how a
novelist persuades us. The rules of this are precisely what literary critics
are interested in. So, if you want to engage in this kind of analysis, one of
the first things you have to do is read something about the relevant area
of literary criticism, and find out how to select and analyse passages that
are typical.

Before we look at the extracts, we need some context from the story.
The passages all relate to events around the battle of Austerlitz, which
was (in actual history) one of the most significant conflicts of the nineteenth century, being the decisive victory for Napoleon's France over
Russia and Austria. Rostov, a young cavalry officer, is a central character
in the novel; Alexander is the Tsar (Emperor):

> The Emperor came level with Rostov and reined in his horse.
> Alexander's face was even more beautiful than it had been at the
> review three days before. It shone with such gaiety and youth – such
> innocent youthfulness that it suggested the high spirits of a boy of
> fourteen – and yet it was still the face of the majestic Emperor.
> Casually glancing up and down the squadron, the Sovereign's eyes
> met Rostov's and for upwards of two seconds rested on them.
> Whether or no the Tsar realised what was going on in Rostov's soul
> (it seemed to Rostov that he saw everything), at any rate for the
> space of two seconds his blue eyes gazed into Rostov's face. A soft
> mild light poured from them. Then all at once he raised his eyebrows,
> and with a sharp movement of his left foot touched his horse and
> galloped on.
>
> (Tolstoy 1957: 294–5)

The key point that Tolstoy is getting across here, and which he elaborates in the following pages, is that Rostov, who is an individual – created as a living individual by Tolstoy with all his powers as a novelist – is coming face-to-face, literally, with history. Tsar Alexander I is a real historical character: he is real history.

As the story develops, Tolstoy tries to dramatise his belief that this type of contact between an individual and history, happening amongst thousands of individuals, creates a collective emotion of military patriotism. For example:

> And Rostov got up and took himself off to wander about among the camp-fires, dreaming of what happiness it would be to die, not saving the Emperor's life (of that he did not even dare dream), but simply to die before his eyes. He really was in love with the Tsar and the glory of the Russian arms and the hope of coming victory. And he was not the only one to experience this feeling during those memorable days that preceded the battle of Austerlitz: nine-tenths of the men in the Russian army were at that moment in love, though perhaps less ecstatically, with their Tsar and the glory of the Russian arms.
>
> (296–7)

This is what the novelist does to encapsulate the question of what we as social scientists would call 'structure and agency'. Agency is in the real individual, Rostov. Structure is in Russia, the nation, embodied in the Tsar at a crucial moment in its history.

The battle takes place and Russia loses, and then Rostov encounters the Tsar again:

> At that moment Alexander turned his head and Rostov saw the beloved features that were so deeply engraved on his memory. The Emperor was pale, his cheeks looked sunken and his eyes hollow, but the charm, the gentleness of his face, was all the more striking. Rostov felt happy in the certainty that the rumours about the Emperor being wounded were false. He was happy to be seeing him. He knew that he might, that indeed he ought to go straight to him and deliver the message Dolgorukov had commanded him to deliver.
>
> But as a youth in love trembles and turns faint and dares not utter what he has spent nights in dreaming of, and looks around in terror, seeking aid or a chance of delay and flight, when the longed-for moment arrives and he is alone with *her*, so Rostov, now that he had attained what he had longed for beyond everything in the world, did not know how to approach the Emperor, and a thousand reasons

occurred to him why it would be untimely, improper and impossible
to do so.

(334)

Even when the Tsar has been defeated, he still remains a historical
figure. He does not become an individual like Rostov. We still have this
dichotomy of structure and agency. Rostov, as an individual, is discovering
that it is not possible to come into direct contact with this remote figure
who embodies history. Indeed, right throughout the novel there is that
dichotomy between the agency of an individual and the intangibility of
history. Tolstoy's use of the extended simile here ('as a youth…') draws on
a very old literary tradition – going back to the ancient Greeks – of
addressing the relationship between the individual and fate through the
epic poem.

In fact, however, Rostov immediately regrets not having talked to the
Tsar. He has not taken advantage of what Tolstoy would call chance. One
of his central themes is that the scope for individuals to influence history
is through chance. This is summed up in the next passage, taken from the
body of the text, but in the style of the theoretical essay at the end:

> Just as in the mechanism of a clock, so in the mechanism of the mili-
> tary machine, an impetus once given leads on to the final result; and
> the parts of the mechanism which have not yet been started into
> action remain as indifferently stationary. Wheels creak on their axles
> as the cogs engage, the revolving pulleys whirr in rapid motion, while
> the next wheel stands as apathetic and still as though it would stay so
> for a hundred years; but the momentum reaches it – the lever catches
> and the wheel, obeying the impulse, creaks and joins in the common
> movement, the result and aim of which are beyond its ken.
>
> (298)

This is an image of society as a vast mechanism – as it were, Tolstoy's
theoretical conclusion from his qualitative research on individuals and
history.

What can we take from this for the use of novels in social research
more generally? First of all, Tolstoy has a certain theme, a problematic as
the social scientist might call it: he wants to look at the relationship
between structure and agency. The battle of Austerlitz is a key example in
which lots of individuals, that is potential agents, come into conflict with
structure, that is history, and most of them have no capacity whatsoever
to influence things. If they are going to have that capacity, they have to

take advantage of it when it occurs by chance as an unpredictable opportunity. This is something that Rostov fails to do.

The difference from what the social scientist might do is the existence
of Rostov. We might write about Tsar Alexander I or the battle of
Austerlitz, and if we were nineteenth-century social scientists we might
write a paragraph like the one about the clock and the cogwheels. But
what we would not be likely to do is attempt to create through language a
fully rounded portrait of an individual human being. That is the unique
contribution of Tolstoy. As well as making it all into a good story, it also
enhances the novel's use as social science. Drawing on literature in this
way is the richest use that we can make of it in social science. Writers of
this sort might actually be better at doing certain things than we are: by
their capacity to create credible individuals they might be better at
achieving validity.

What is more, the success of good novelists does not depend at all on
questions of representativeness. In fact, one of the most long-standing
debates in literary criticism concerns precisely whether representativeness
is relevant at all. For example, many people have argued that Jane Austen
is very revealing about eighteenth-century England, even though she
almost never mentions war at a time when most of Europe was engulfed in
wars. Edward Said has argued, further, that her novels – especially
Mansfield Park – reflect Britain's emerging imperial role (Said 1993:
100–116). Similarly, say, with Marcel Proust's writing in *A La Recherche du
Temps Perdu*: you could crudely characterise his novel as a description of
upper-class literati in late nineteenth-century Paris, most of whom were
also homosexual. Put like that, it seems almost as unrepresentative as you
could imagine. But, on the other hand, the novel is one of the most
telling accounts of social change and of politics that has been written this
past century. So the persuasiveness of the novel does not depend on its
characters' being representative.

What makes the potential for using novels even more interesting and
complicated is that novelists themselves often reflect on the process of
storytelling and the deliberate lying that goes into making the stories
truer. Here is a final extract from *War and Peace*:

> He began his story with the intention of telling everything exactly as
> it happened, but imperceptibly, unconsciously and inevitably he
> passed into falsehood. If he had told the truth to his listeners who,
> like himself, had heard numerous descriptions of cavalry charges and
> had formed a definite idea of what a charge was like and were
> expecting a precisely similar account from him, either they would not
> have believed him, or, worse still, would have thought Rostov himself

to blame if what generally happens to those who describe cavalry charges had not happened to him. He could not tell them simply that they had all set out at a trot, that he had fallen off his horse, sprained his arm and then run from the Frenchmen into the woods as fast as his legs would carry him. Besides, to tell everything exactly as it had been would have meant the exercise of considerable self-control to confine himself to the facts. It is very difficult to tell the truth and young people are rarely capable of it. His listeners expected to hear how, forgetful of himself and all on fire with excitement, he had rushed down like a hurricane on the enemy's square, hacked his way in, slashing the French right and left; how his sabre had tasted flesh, and he had fallen exhausted, and so on. And that was what he told them.

(279)

The argument here is that there was something true in Rostov's account despite the fact that it was factually false. The persuasive power of these writings depends not on the representativeness but on the quality of the insights.

If there is a question of representativeness, it has something to do with cultural representativeness. A useful approach can be through structural linguistics. The idea is that writers distil the messages that are already inscribed in the language as a whole, and insofar as these linguistic codes embody the spirit of the times, then writers can give us unique access to that spirit. This contradicts the common sense assumption that novels are about life, written from personal experience which is the source of their authenticity. Common sense, the average reader may say, is that really good novels tell truths and express the individual insights of their authors. The contrary view is then that all text, be it social scientific or novel, has to be read independently from its author. This view argues that the world is intelligible only through discourse: there is no unmediated experience. We cannot access the raw reality of our own and others' selves. Texts come to take on multiple meanings, and the object of a critic is to seek not the unity of a work but the multiplicity of its meanings, its omissions and its contradictions. This view of text corresponds fairly closely to that of the playwright Bertolt Brecht, who arrived at it without the aid of modern criticism. It asks the reader to confront contradiction; the classic realist view of text is to efface it.

If you go along with this view of the novel, then it seems at first glance that we cannot treat novels and plays as doing more than raise questions; we have to ask questions of the text to obtain answers. The sting in the tail, however, comes if we are reflexive about it and ask whether our own social scientific texts are similarly plural. At the very moment when some literary critics are moving in this direction in their understanding of all text, some social scientists wish to foreground the author's unique voice, and make explicit their idiosyncratic values, politics, and so on. Perhaps acknowledging the pluralism even of social scientific texts would be a rather more productive line to pursue.

Whatever the resolution among these theoretical positions, all would agree that imaginative literature can help us to understand the things we are studying, allowing us (and our readers) access to multiple meanings, and enriching the meaning through making explicit the variety of interpretations any assemblage of data can bear. An example of this use is from a study by Diana Forsythe and colleagues of small schools in rural Scotland (Forsythe 1983). This was a multi-disciplinary investigation, sponsored by a government agency, and involving educationalists, sociologists, historians and economists. The research found ambivalence among rural people in their attitudes to their communities – attachment to tradition and community, associated with family and with Scottish identity, but also frustration at the parochialism and the lack of employment opportunity. In parallel with this, they also found an ambivalence between particularism and the universalism that could come from education. The researchers documented all that with the usual academic care and rigour, but chose to sum it up from a novel about social change in rural Scotland. They quote a passage from *Sunset Song* by Lewis Grassic Gibbon, which is about the passing of one type of rural community in the face of unavoidable historical change. It, too – like *War and Peace* – is partly about the tension between structure and agency, and about the ambivalent desire of its central character, Chris Guthrie, to escape from history and yet also remain attached to her community. Its narrative passages are written in a style that draws on the language of rural North-East Scotland where it is set, and part of the contrast that is being drawn is also between that language and the English language of formal education (which is also, for us, the language of social research):

> So that was Chris and her reading and schooling, two Chrisses there were that fought for her heart and tormented her. You hated the land and the coarse speak of the folk and learning was brave and fine one day; and the next you'd waken with the peewits [lapwings] crying across the hills, deep and deep, crying in the heart of you and the smell of the earth in your face, almost you'd cry for that, the beauty of it and the sweetness of the Scottish land and skies. You saw their faces in firelight, father's and mother's and the neighbours', before the

lamps lit up, tired and kind, faces dear and close to you, you wanted the words they'd known and used, forgotten in the far-off youngness of their lives, Scots words to tell to your heart how they wrung it and held it, the toil of their days and unendingly their fight. And the next minute that passed from you, you were English, back to the English words so sharp and clean and true – for a while, for a while, till they slid so smooth from your throat you knew they could never say anything that was worth saying at all.

(Grassic Gibbon 1971: 35–6)

As the research authors comment:

There can be no tidy recommendation about whether or not to keep small primary schools in rural Scotland, because an examination of the place of the rural school is not a circumscribed technical exercise capable of generating a tidy recommendation.

(Forsythe 1983: 210)

So, because novelists have skills that can represent both individuals and structures, they are a safeguard against the danger for social research of losing sight of individuals amidst the structure and the theory. In the words of the literary critic Cairns Craig, writing about historians but with obvious implications for social science,

the historian can only 'compose' a history about events which have a 'composed' order; but what this means is that there is always something else beyond the boundaries of…*composed* history, a *counter-historical* flux of human events.

(Craig 1996: 68, original emphasis)

He argues that good novelists – and he is dealing particularly here with Walter Scott – show this tension because of the contrast between the specificity of individual characters (such as Rostov or Chris Guthrie) and the structures of historical change embodied in the narrative.

We are asking the novelist and the good journalist to imbue events with meaning. And the reason we want to do that is summed up by the sociologist Philip Abrams (1982). An event, he argues, is not just a happening. It is 'a happening to which cultural significance has success-fully been assigned' (191). Abrams is mainly concerned with arguing that sociology and history are both necessary disciplines for assigning cultural significance to events. But neither they nor any single academic discipline is sufficient. The argument of this chapter has been that journalists and imaginative writers are a type of social researcher. They may give us rather better qualitative evidence than we can generate ourselves. They, like us, are ultimately also concerned with attaching cultural significance to events.

Guide to further reading

General

Most books with 'research design' or something like it in their titles turn out to focus on experimental methods and on hypothesis testing. An exception is Hakim (1987). We do not know of a book which reflects the approach and philosophy of the present one. However, there are also a few publications in which authors discuss how they actually did the research. Obviously, these are accounts by participants rather than independent descriptions, and have to be treated as such, but they are of considerable interest. See for instance Bell and Newby (1977), Bell and Encel (1978), Hammond (1964) and Platt (1976).

Experiments

The view that experiments are a paradigm which ought to be followed as far as possible is expressed quite widely, for example by Bulmer (1986b: 155–79), Fitz-Gibbon (1988), Moser and Kalton (1985), Oakley and Fullerton (1996), Sobel (1996) and Stouffer (1950). That view is doubted by, for example, Goldstein and Blatchford (1998) and Willer and Willer (1973). Except in psychology and medicine (e.g. Breakwell et al. 1995), extensive discussion of experiments is rare in books intended for social scientists, but it can be found in economics, especially on the economic behaviour of individuals (Davis and Holt 1993) and in some other areas of policy research (Boruch 1997). The random fluctuations to be found in small experiments are illustrated by Goldstein and Blatchford (1998: 258). The notion of quasi-experiments has gained some acceptance in social science: a very full discussion is provided by Cook and Campbell (1979), and more recent discussion of applications can be found in Boruch (1997) and Oakley and Roberts (1996). The epistemological issues underlying these debates are explored by Goldthorpe (1998), Hacking (1983) and

Hage and Meeker (1988). The specific epistemological issues concerning the example in the Appendix to Chapter 2 are discussed by Hacking (1975; 1983). The problems of intervention are discussed by Oakley and Roberts (1996). Multivariate statistical methods to allow for threats to validity are discussed in many books; just one example is Bryman and Cramer (1997). Action research is dealt with by Cohen and Manion (1994).

Representativeness

Trying to establish that empirical conclusions can be generalised is so central to social research that most books on research design and method discuss it, although the flavour of the discussion will depend on the discipline involved. Quantitative methods emphasise the technology of representative sampling (e.g. Moser and Kalton 1985; Marsh 1982). Qualitative methods emphasise judgement (Dey 1993). The philosophical issues are addressed by the contributors to the book edited by Bulmer (1991), and – for those with some understanding of the mathematics involved – there is an exceptionally clear discussion by Smith (1976), and in the discussion of that paper which is printed alongside it. Smith (1983) discusses the conditions under which inferences drawn from non-random samples are valid. The role of sample size is assessed by, for example, Groves (1989: 245–6) and Moser and Kalton (1985: 146). The origins of sampling are outlined by Bulmer (1991), Hacking (1990) and Mackenzie (1981). Stratification and clustering are discussed in all good-quality books on sampling: some notable examples are Hoinville and Jowell (1977) and Kalton (1983). The analysis of such surveys can become highly complex, but great advances in the technology for doing so have been made in recent years: see, for example, Goldstein (1995) and Skinner *et al.* (1989).

Choice of locale and group

The choice of locale and group is intrinsic to every empirical study. The best way to learn to design research in these terms is to become thoroughly familiar with the empirical literature in relevant fields, paying special attention to the way the researchers choose the locale and group and the reasons they give for this. The accounts of research mentioned above in the General section of this list of further reading are a good place to start.

Case studies can take many forms. There is a categorisation of case studies in Hakim (1987). For a sophisticated dicussion of these issues see Ragin and Becker (1992).

A useful brief introduction to case studies is Stake (1994). A short account which locates case studies in various intellectual traditions is Hamel *et al.* (1993). The most frequently referred to book on the subject is Yin (1994) (a revised edition of an earlier work) and, on their more applied aspects, Yin (1993).

Interviews and alternatives

For an excellent overview of the use of images, which traces the transition from images as able to reveal the truth, through a more analytic period which saw them as reflecting chosen aspects of reality, to modern and postmodern positions, see Harper (1994). A useful brief account of the use of photographs is Ball and Smith (1992).

Those interested in the use of secondary analysis should consult Dale *et al.* (1988), Hakim (1982) or Kiecolt and Nathan (1985). An indication of the wealth of material available can be gained from the Data Archive website at http://dawww.essex.ac.uk or the website and newsletter of Social and Commmunity Planning Research (SCPR) at http://www.scpr.ac.uk For information on the archiving of qualitative data consult the website of the Qualidata group in the Department of Sociology at the University of Essex (http://www.essex.ac.uk/qualidata).

Information on the Sample of Anonymised Records is easily obtained from the website of the Cathie Marsh Centre for Survey and Census Research at the University of Manchester (http://les.man.ac.uk/ccsr) which also contains a list of publications using the data.

There is a vast number of books on interviewing in general. For a recent introductory overview of the 'qualitative interview' with many useful references, see Fontana and Frey (1994). Kahn and Cannell (1957) is an old but still valuable discussion. Mishler (1986) is by a social psychologist who discusses taking reflexivity and the nature of the inter-action into account when analysing interview data.

The early use of the focused interview by Merton and Kendall led to the production of a manual which more than forty years later remains a valuable practical guide: see Merton *et al.* (1956). The group interview, especially the focus group, has been extensively discussed in recent years. Useful starting points are Morgan (1997) and Stewart (1990), which are referred to in the text. Frey and Oishi (1995) is a recent and very practical account of how to conduct interviews, especially useful for its discussion of telephone intervewing, which is being increasingly widely used.

Structured questionnaires

Any book on social surveys devotes attention to how to design and ask questions – for example, Belson (1981), Converse and Presser (1986), Hoinville and Jowell (1977), Moser and Kalton (1985) and Munn and Drever (1990). The classic account by Payne (1951) is still worth reading. Much sensible insight into how interviewers use structured questionnaires can be found in the practical handbook prepared by UK government statisticians for people working on official social surveys (McCrossan 1991). Research on this topic has burgeoned in recent decades: an authoritative summary is provided by Groves (1989), and further discussion can be found in the newsletter of SCPR, London (website: http://www.scpr.ac.uk/). Research on how to overcome some of the difficulties of question wording is summarised by SCPR (1996b), Groves (1989) and Converse and Presser (1986). Questionnaires for postal surveys are discussed in SCPR (1996a). The 1997 election survey is documented on the website at http://www.strath.ac.uk/Other/CREST/. SCPR (1996b) provides a report of a recent conference on models of response, and Belson (1981) gives a comprehensive discussion.

Fieldwork

There is a vast literature on fieldwork of all kinds. For an excellent brief introduction, with many useful references, see Atkinson and Hammersley (1994). See also Hammersley and Atkinson (1995) for a much more extended account. Burgess (1991) is a reprint of a well-known work on sociological fieldwork. Spradley (1980) is an account of fieldwork from a more anthropological perspective, and for an account of the use of the interview in the fieldwork situation see Spradley (1979).

Anthropologists by virtue of their training will be familiar with the specialist literature in the field; those coming from other disciplines can use the literature mentioned here and in the text as a starting point, but should refer to the specialist monographs in their area of interest. The literature on the nature of the authorial voice and the politics of ethnography is relevant to those of all disciplines wishing to do fieldwork. See for instance Clifford and Marcus (1986) and Van Maanen (1988).

Lee (1994) is an unusual book in that it brings home to the inexperienced researcher that fieldwork is not without risk.

Time

An excellent text on the analysis of quantitative data over time, based on examples, is Dale and Davies (1994). Menard (1991) is a useful brief introduction.

Information about the cohort studies is conveniently obtained from the website of the Centre for Longitudinal Studies at the Institute of Education, University of London (http://cls.ioe.ac.uk). The site also contains a list of publications using the data. A preliminary account of the findings of the fifth sweep of the National Child Development Study can be found in Ferri (1993).

An account of the British Household Panel Study is also to be found on the World Wide Web at http://www.iser.essex.ac.uk/bhps and includes a list of some publications which have resulted from the study and an account of research under way.

The handbook for the 1991 Census by Dale and Marsh (1993) includes a section on the Office of Population Censuses and Surveys Longitudinal Study by Dale.

A valuable introduction to oral history by one of the leading enthusiasts for the method is Thompson (1988).

A useful brief introduction to various aspects of biography and autobiography is the special issue of the journal *Sociology*, 'Auto/Biography', 27, 1, February 1993. See also Atkinson (1998).

For those wishing to learn more about the life history, Daniel Bertaux's edited book *Biography and Society* (1981) is a good place to start, and the journal *Life Stories* or *Récits de Vie*, now *The International Yearbook of Oral History and Life Studies*, is a testament to the growth of interest in this research approach. See also Plummer (1983) and Denzin (1988).

Policy research

There was much discussion in the 1970s and 1980s about the role of research in social policy: notable examples are Booth (1988), Bulmer (1986a), Gordon *et al.* (1977), Kallen *et al.* (1982), Lindblom and Cohen (1979), Majchrzak (1984) and Weiss (1977b; 1986). This activity has abated somewhat, although any thorough piece of policy research reports on the issues of design with which it had to deal. There has been some discussion recently of the specific problems raised by evaluation research (Boruch 1997; Oakley and Roberts 1996). The capacity of research to set the terms of debate is assessed by Bulmer (1986b: 178), Dale (1994) and Rein and Schon (1977: 235). Hakim's idea of theoretical research is developed from Majchrzak (1984). The role of experiments in giving validity to policy research is explored thoroughly by Boruch (1997). The role of research in a democracy is discussed by Knox and McAlister (1995).

Journalism and literature

There has been less systematic discussion of the topics in this chapter than of any of the other themes in the book. Scott (1990) deals with the general topic of using documents, and the particular research projects cited in the chapter do reflect on how they used literature. Any book on qualitative research addresses the question of selecting quotations from interviewees to illustrate the discussion of research findings, and something like the same considerations would be relevant to selecting material from other illustrative sources, such as novels or newspapers. For example, Dey (1993: 237–63) provides a thorough and helpful discussion of how to construct an account of some social phenomenon from the qualitative data. The political controversies surrounding educational research are exemplified in Tooley and Darby (1998). Styles of nineteenth-century social science are discussed by Thompson (1978). Structure and agency are the topic of Abrams (1982). Structural linguistics is explained in Culler (1975) and Belsey (1980).

Bibliography

Abel-Smith, B. and Townsend, P. (1965) *The Poor and the Poorest: A New Analysis of the Ministry of Labour's Family Expenditure Surveys of 1953–4 and 1960*, London: G. Bell.

Abrams, P. (1982) *Historical Sociology*, London: Shepton Mallet.

Anderson, M., Bechhofer, F. and Gershuny, J. (eds) (1994) *The Social and Political Economy of the Household*, Oxford: Oxford University Press.

Anderson, Nels (1923) *The Hobo: The Sociology of the Homeless Man*, Chicago: University of Chicago Press.

Atkinson, P. and Hammersley, M. (1994) 'Ethnography and participant observation', in Norman K. Denzin and Yvonna S. Lincoln (eds) *Handbook of Qualitative Research*, London: Sage, 248–61.

Atkinson, Robert (1998) *The Life Story Interview*, London: Sage.

Ball, M. S. and Smith, G. W. H. (1992) *Analyzing Visual Data*, London: Sage.

Ball, S. (1988) 'Unintended effects in educational research', in J. Keeves (ed.) *Educational Research, Methodology and Measurement: An International Handbook*, Oxford: Pergamon, 490–3.

Bateson, G. and Mead, M. (1942) *Balinese Character: A Photographic Analysis*, New York: The New York Academy of Sciences.

Bechhofer, F., Elliott, B. and McCrone, D. (1984) 'Safety in numbers: on the use of multiple interviewers', *Sociology*, 18, 1, 97–101.

Bechhofer, F., McCrone, D., Kiely, R. and Stewart, R. (1999) 'Constructing national identity: arts and landed elites in Scotland', *Sociology* 33, 3, 515–34.

Becker, Howard S. (1961) *Boys in White: Student Culture in Medical School*, Chicago: University of Chicago Press.

Bell, C. and Encel, S. (eds) (1978) *Inside the Whale*, Oxford: Pergamon.

Bell, C. and Howieson, C. (1988) 'The view from the hutch: educational guinea pigs speak about TVEI', in D. Raffe (ed.) *Education and the Youth Labour Market*, London: Falmer, 222–42.

Bell, C., Howieson, C., King, K. and Raffe, D. (1989) 'The Scottish dimension of TVEI', in A. Brown and D. McCrone (eds) *Scottish Government Yearbook*, Edinburgh: Unit for the Study of Government in Scotland, 92–103.

Bell, C. and Newby, H. (eds) (1977) *Doing Sociological Research*, London: Allen and Unwin.

Belsey, C. (1980) *Critical Practice*, London: Methuen.

Belson, W. A. (1981) *The Design and Understanding of Survey Questions*, Aldershot: Gower.

Bertaux, Daniel (ed.) (1981) *Biography and Society: The Life History Approach in the Social Sciences*, Beverley Hills: Sage.

Billig, Michael (1995) *Banal Nationalism*, London: Sage.

Blatchford, P. and Martin, C. (1998) 'The effects of class size on classroom processes', *British Journal of Educational Studies*, 46, 2, 118–37.

Blatchford, P. and Mortimore, P. (1994) 'The issue of class size for young children in schools: what can we learn from research?', *Oxford Review of Education*, 20, 4, 411–28.

Booth, T. (1988) *Developing Policy Research*, Aldershot: Avebury.

Boruch, R. F. (1997) *Randomised Experiments for Planning and Evaluation*, London: Sage.

Bowker, Graham (1993) 'The age of biography is upon us', *Times Higher Educational Supplement*, 8 January, 19.

Breakwell, G., Hammond, S. and Fife-Shaw, C. (eds) (1995) *Research Methods in Psychology*, London: Sage.

Brown, A., McCrone, D. and Paterson, L. (1998) *Politics and Society in Scotland*, 2nd edn, London: Macmillan.

Brown, A., McCrone, D., Paterson, L. and Surridge, P. (1999) *The Scottish Electorate*, Basingstoke: Macmillan.

Brown, S. and McIntyre, D. (1993) *Making Sense of Teaching*, Buckingham: Open University Press.

Bryman, A. and Cramer, D. (1997) *Quantitative Data Analysis*, London: Routledge.

Buck, N., Gershuny, J., Rose, D. and Scott, J. (1994) *Changing Households: The BHPS 1990–2*, Colchester: ESRC Research Centre on Micro-Social Change, University of Essex.

Bulmer, M. (1986b) 'Evaluation, research and social experimentation', in M. Bulmer (ed.) *Social Science and Social Policy*, London: Allen and Unwin, 155–79.

——(1986c) 'The policy process and the place in it of social research', in M. Bulmer (ed.) *Social Science and Social Policy*, London: Allen and Unwin, 3–30.

Bulmer, M. (ed.) (1986a) *Social Science and Social Policy*, London: Allen and Unwin.

——(1991) *The Social Survey in Historical Perspective*, Cambridge: Cambridge University Press.

Burawoy, Michael (1979) *Manufacturing Consent: Changes in the Labor Process under Monopoly Capitalism*, Chicago: University of Chicago Press.

Burgess, Robert G. (1991) *In the Field*, London: Allen and Unwin.

Burnhill, P. (1984) 'The ragged edge of compulsory schooling', in D. Raffe (ed.) *Fourteen to Eighteen*, Aberdeen: Aberdeen University Press, 79–103.

Burnhill, P., McPherson, A., Raffe, D. and Tomes, N. (1987) 'Constructing a public account of an education system', in G. Walford (ed.) *Doing Sociology of Education*, Lewes: Falmer, 207–29.

Burns, T. (1977) *The BBC: Public Institution and Private World*, London: Macmillan.

Burtless, G. and Greenberg, D. (1982) 'Inferences concerning labor supply behaviour based on limited-duration experiments', *American Economic Review*, 72, 488–97.

Butler, D. and Kavanagh, D. (1997) *The British General Election of 1997*, London: Macmillan.

Campbell, B. (1987) *Iron Ladies: Why do Women Vote Tory?*, London: Virago.

Cannell, C. F., Miller, P. V. and Oksenberg, L. (1981) 'Research on interviewing techniques', in S. Leinhardt (ed.) *Sociological Methodology 1981*, San Francisco: Jossey-Bass, 389–437.

Canner, P. L. (1987) 'An overview of six clinical trials of aspirin in coronary heart disease', *Statistics in Medicine*, 6, 255–63.

Christy, C. A. (1987) *Sex Differences in Political Participation*, New York: Praeger.

Clifford, J. and Marcus, G. E. (eds) (1986) *Writing Ethnography: The Poetics and Politics of Ethnography*, Berkeley: University of California Press.

Cockburn, C. (1983) *Brothers: Male Dominance and Technological Change*, London: Pluto.

Cohen, Anthony P. (1987) *Whalsay: Symbol, Segment and Boundary in a Shetland Island Community*, Manchester: Manchester University Press.

Cohen, L. and Manion, L. (1994) *Research Methods in Education*, 4th edn, London: Routledge.

Coleman, James S. (1990) *Foundations of Social Theory*, Cambridge, MA: The Belknap Press of Harvard University Press.

Converse, J. M. and Presser, S. (1986) *Survey Questions: Handcrafting the Standardised Questionnaire*, London: Sage.

Converse, P. (1964) 'The nature of belief systems in mass publics', in D. Apter (ed.) *Ideology and Discontent*, New York: Free Press, 206–61.

Cook, T. D. and Campbell, D. T. (1979) *Quasi-Experimentation: Design and Analysis Issues For Field Settings*, Chicago: Rand McNally.

Coxon, A. P. M. and Davies, P. M. with Jones, C. L. (1986) *Images of Social Stratification: Occupational Structures and Class*, London: Sage.

Craig, C. (1996) *Out of History*, Edinburgh: Polygon.

Culler, J. (1975) *Structuralist Poetics: Structuralism, Linguistics and the Study of Literature*, London: Routledge and Kegan Paul.

Curtice, J. and Jowell, R. (1998) 'Is there really a demand for constitutional change?', in L. Paterson (ed.) *Understanding Constitutional Change*, special issue of *Scottish Affairs*, 61–92.

Dale, A. and Davies, R. B. (eds) (1994) *Analysing Social and Political Change*, London: Sage.

Dale, A., Arber, S. and Proctor, M. (1988) *Doing Secondary Analysis*, London: Unwin Hyman.

Dale, A. and Marsh, C. (eds) (1993) *The Census User's Handbook*, London: HMSO.

Dale, R. (1994) 'Applied education politics or political sociology of education? Contrasting approaches to the study of recent education reform in England and Wales', in D. Halpin and B. Troyna (eds) *Researching Educational Policy*, London: Falmer, 31–41.

Davis, D. and Holt, C. (1993) *Experimental Economics*, Princeton: Princeton University Press.

Denzin, N. K. (1970) *The Research Act*, London: Butterworths.

——(1988) *Interpretive Biography*, London: Sage.

Denzin, N. K. and Lincoln, Y. S. (eds) (1994) *Handbook of Qualitative Research*, London: Sage.

Dey, I. (1993) *Qualitative Data Analysis*, London: Routledge.

Donaldson, W. (1986) *Popular Literature in Victorian Scotland*, Aberdeen: Aberdeen University Press.

Douglas, J. W. B. (1964) *The Home and the School*, London: MacGibbon and Kee.

Dunaway, D. K. and Baum, W. K. (1997) *Oral History: An Interdisciplinary Anthology*, London: Sage.

Elias, P. and Main, B. (1982) *Women's Working Lives: Evidence from the National Training Survey*, Coventry: University of Warwick, Institute for Employment Research.

Ellegård, A. (1958) *Darwin and the General Reader*, Gothenburg: Gothenburg Studies in English.

Elliott, H. (1997) 'The use of diaries in sociological research on health experience', *Sociological Research Online*, 2, 2 (http://www.socresonline.org.uk/socresonline/2/2/7.html).

Esmail, A. and Everington, S. (1993) 'Racial discrimination against doctors from ethnic minorities', *British Medical Journal*, 306, 13 March, 691–2.

Fenton, J. (1988) *All the Wrong Places: Adrift in the Politics of Asia*, Harmondsworth: Penguin.

Ferri, Elsa (ed.) (1993) *Life at 33: The Fifth Follow-up of the National Child Development Study*, London: National Children's Bureau.

Finch, Janet (1993) '"It's great to have someone to talk to": ethics and politics of interviewing women', in M. Hammersley (ed.) (1993) *Social Research: Philosophy, Politics, and Practice*, London: Sage, 166–80.

Finn, D. (1987) *Training Without Jobs: New Deals and Broken Promises*, London: Macmillan.

Finn, J. D. and Achilles, C. M. (1990) 'Answers and questions about class size: a statewide experiment', *American Educational Research Journal*, 27, 557–77.

Fitz-Gibbon, C. (1988) 'Learning from unwelcome data: lessons from the TVEI examination results', in D. Hopkins (ed.) *TVEI at the Change of Life*, Clevedon: Multi-Lingual Matters, 92–101.

Floud, J. E., Halsey, A. H. and Martin, F. M. (1956) *Social Class and Educational Opportunity*, London: Heinemann.

Fontana, A. and Frey, J. (1994) 'Interviewing: the art of science', in N. K. Denzin and Y. S. Lincoln (eds) *Handbook of Qualitative Research*, London: Sage, 361–76.

Forsythe, D. (1983) *The Rural Community and the Small School*, Aberdeen: Aberdeen University Press.

Fraser, H., Draper, J. and Taylor, W. (1998) 'The quality of teachers' professional lives: teachers and job satisfaction', *Evaluation and Research in Education*, 12, 2, 61–71.

Frey, J. H. and Oishi, S. M. (1995) *How to Conduct Interviews by Telephone and in Person*, London: Sage.

Fulton, M., Raab, G., Thomson, G., Laxen, D., Hunter, R. and Hepburn, W. (1987) 'Influence of blood lead on the ability and attainment of children in Edinburgh', *The Lancet*, 30 May, 1221–5.

Gamoran, A. (1992) 'Is ability grouping equitable?', *Educational Leadership*, 50, October, 11–17.

Garfinkel, Harold (1967) *Studies in Ethnomethodology*, Englewood Cliffs: Prentice-Hall.

Gershuny, J. and Robinson, J. (1988) 'Historical changes in the household division of labour', *Demography*, 25, 4, 537–52.

Gershuny, J., Godwin, M. and Jones, S. (1994) 'The domestic labour revolution: a process of lagged adaptation', in M. Anderson, F. Bechhofer and J. Gershuny (eds) *The Social and Political Economy of the Household*, Oxford: Oxford University Press, 151–97.

Giddens, A. (1991) *Modernity and Self-Identity*, Cambridge: Polity.

Glaser, B. G. and Strauss, A. L. (1967) *The Discovery of Grounded Theory*, New York: Aldine de Gruyter.

Glass, D. V. (ed.) (1954) *Social Mobility in Britain*, London: Routledge and Kegan Paul.

Gleeson, D. (ed.) (1987) *TVEI and Secondary Education*, Milton Keynes: Open University Press.

Goffman, Erving (1979) *Gender Advertisements*, London: Macmillan.

Gold, R. (1958) 'Roles in sociological field observations', *Social Forces*, 36, 217–23.

Goldstein, H. (1995) *Multilevel Statistical Models*, 2nd edn, London: Edward Arnold.

Goldstein, H. and Blatchford, P. (1998) 'Class size and educational achievement: a review of methodology with particular reference to study design', *British Educational Research Journal*, 24, 3, 255–67.

Goldthorpe, J. H. (1998) 'Causation, statistics and sociology', Twenty Ninth Geary Lecture, Dublin: Economic and Social Research Institute.

Goldthorpe, J. H., Lockwood, D., Bechhofer, F. and Platt, J. (1969) *The Affluent Worker in the Class Structure*, Cambridge: Cambridge University Press.

Gordon, I., Lewis, J. and Young, K. (1977) 'Perspectives on policy analysis', *Public Administration Bulletin*, 25, 26–35.

Gould, S. J. (1981) *The Mismeasure of Man*, New York: Norton.

Gow, L. and McPherson, A. (1980) *Tell Them From Me*, Aberdeen: Aberdeen University Press.

Grassic Gibbon, Lewis (1971) *Sunset Song*, London: Longman.

Groves, R. M. (1989) *Survey Errors and Survey Costs*, New York: Wiley.

Hacking, I. (1975) *The Emergence of Probability*, Cambridge: Cambridge University Press.

——(1983) *Representing and Intervening*, Cambridge: Cambridge University Press.

——(1990) *The Taming of Chance*, Cambridge: Cambridge University Press.

Hage, J. and Meeker, B. F. (1988) *Social Causality*, London: Unwin Hyman.

Hakim, C. (1982) *Secondary Analysis in Social Research: A Guide to Data Sources and Methods with Examples*, London: Allen and Unwin.

——(1987) [1977] *Research Design*, 2nd edn, London: Routledge.

Hall, R. L. and Hitch, C. (1951) 'Price theory and business behaviour', in T. Wilson and P. W. S. Andrews (eds) *Oxford Studies in the Price Mechanism*, Oxford: Oxford University Press, 107–38.

Hallam, S. and Toutounji, I. (1996) *What Do We Know about the Grouping of Pupils by Ability?*, London: Institute of Education.

Hamel, J., Dufour, S. and Fortin, D. (1993) *Case Study Methods*, London: Sage.

Hammersley, M. and Atkinson, P. (1995) *Ethnography: Principles and Practice*, London: Routledge.

Hammersley, M. (ed.) (1993) *Social Research: Philosophy, Politics, and Practice*, London: Sage.

Hammond, P. E. (ed.) (1964) *Sociologists at Work*, New York: Basic Books.

Harlen, W. and Malcolm, H. (1997) *Setting and Streaming: A Research Review*, Edinburgh: Scottish Council for Research in Education.

Harper, Douglas (1994) 'On the authority of the image: visual methods at the crossroads', in N. K. Denzin and Y. S. Lincoln (eds) *Handbook of Qualitative Research*, London: Sage, 403–12.

Hattersley, L. and Creeser, R. (1995) *Longitudinal Study 1971–91: History, Organisation and Quality of Data*, London: HMSO.

Heath, A., Jowell, R., Curtice, J. and Taylor, B. (1994) *Labour's Last Chance?*, Aldershot: Gower.

Hogwood, B. W. and Gunn, L. A. (1984) *Policy Analysis for the Real World*, Oxford: Oxford University Press.

Hoinville, G. and Jowell, R. (eds) (1977) *Survey Research Practice*, Aldershot: Gower.

Hough, Michael (1995) *Anxiety about Crime: Findings from the 1994 British Crime Survey*, Home Office Research Study 147, London: HMSO.

Hunter, James (1994) *A Dance Called America: The Scottish Highlands, the United States and Canada*, Edinburgh: Mainstream.

Inglehart, R. (1990) *Culture Shift in Advanced Industrial Society*, Princeton: Princeton University Press.

Jeffery, P., Jeffery, R. and Lyon, A. (1989) *Labour Pains and Labour Power: Women and Childbearing in India*, London: Zed Books.

Jeffery, R. and Jeffery, P. (1997) *Population, Gender and Politics: Demographic Change in Rural North India*, Cambridge: Cambridge University Press.

Jordan, A. G. and Richardson, J. J. (1987) *British Politics and the Policy Process*, London: Allen and Unwin.

Jowell, R., Curtice, J., Park, A., Brook, L., Thomson, K. and Bryson, C. (eds) (1997) *British Social Attitudes: The 14th Report*, Aldershot: Ashgate.

Jowell, R., Witherspoon, S. and Brook, L. (eds) (1986) *British Social Attitudes: The 5th Report*, Aldershot: Gower.

Kahn, R. and Cannell, C. F. (1957) *The Dynamics of Interviewing*, New York: Wiley.

Kallen, D. B. P., Kosse, G. B., Wagenaar, H. C., Kloprogge, J. J. J. and Vorbeck, M. (eds) (1982) *Social Science Research and Public Policy Making*, Windsor: NFER-Nelson.

Kalton, G. (1983) *Introduction to Survey Sampling*, London: Sage.

Kalton, G., Collins, M. and Brook, L. (1978) 'Experiments in question wording', *Applied Statistics*, 27, 2, 149–61.

Keeley, M. C., Robins, P. K. and Spiegelman, R. G. (1978) 'The estimation of labor supply models using experimental data', *American Economic Review*, 68, 5, 873–87.

Kelly, A. (ed.) (1987) *Science for Girls?*, Milton Keynes: Open University Press.

Kiecolt, J. and Nathan, L. E. (1985) *Secondary Analysis of Survey Data*, London: Sage.

Knox, C. and McAlister, D. (1995) 'Policy evaluation: incorporating users' views', *Public Administration*, 73, autumn, 413–36.

Kurtz, M. and Spiegelman, R. (1971) 'The Seattle experiment: the combined effect of income maintenance and manpower investments', *American Economic Review Proceedings*, 61, 22–9.

Lazarsfeld, P. F., Berelson, B. and Gaudet, H. (1948) *The People's Choice: How the Voter Makes Up His Mind in a Presidential Campaign*, 2nd edn, New York: Columbia University Press.

Le Roy Ladurie, E. (1978) *Montaillou*, London: Scolar.

Lee, Raymond M. (1994) *Dangerous Fieldwork*, London: Sage.

Lindblom, C. (1980) *The Policy-Making Process*, 2nd edn, Englewood Cliffs: Prentice-Hall.

——(1988) *Democracy and Market System*, Oslo: Norwegian University Press.

Lindblom, C. and Cohen, D. (1979) *Usable Knowledge*, New Haven: Yale University Press.

Lovenduski, J. and Norris, P. (1993) *Gender and Party Politics*, London: Sage.

Lukács, G. (1962) *The Historical Novel*, London: Merlin Press.

Mackenzie, D. (1981) *Statistics in Britain, 1865–1930: The Social Construction of Scientific Knowledge*, Edinburgh: Edinburgh University Press.

Main, B. G. M. (1993) 'Pay in the boardroom: practices and procedures', *Personnel Review*, 22, 7, 1–14.

——(1994) 'The nominations process and corporate governance: a missing link', *Corporate Governance*, 2, 3, 161–9.

Main, B. G. M. and Park, A. (1998) 'An experiment with two-way offers into court: restoring the balance in pre-trial negotiation', available at website http://www.ed.ac.uk/~ejaa17

Majchrzak, A. (1984) *Methods for Policy Research*, London: Sage.

Malinowski, Bronislaw (1922) *Argonauts of the Western Pacific: An Account of Native Enterprise and Adventure in the Archipelagoes of Melanesia*, London: Routledge.

Market Research Society (1994) *The Opinion Polls and the 1992 General Election*, London: Market Research Society.

Marsh, C. (1982) *The Survey Method*, London: Allen and Unwin.

Martin, J. and Roberts, C. (1984) *Women and Employment: A Lifetime Perspective*, report of the 1980 DE/OPCS Women and Employment Survey, London: HMSO.

Mayhew, P., Maung, N. A. and Mirrlees-Black, C. (1993) *The 1992 British Crime Survey*, Home Office Research Study 132, London: HMSO.

McCall, G. J. and Simmons, J. L. (eds) (1969) *Issues in Participant Observation: A Text and Reader*, Reading, MA: Addison-Wesley.

McCrone, D., Kendrick, S. and Straw, P. (eds) (1989) *The Making of Scotland*, Edinburgh: Edinburgh University Press.

McCrone, D., Stewart, R., Kiely, R. and Bechhofer, F. (1998) 'Who are we?: problematising national identity', *Sociological Review*, 46, 4, 629–52.

McCrossan, L. (1991) *A Handbook for Interviewers*, 3rd edn, London: HMSO.

McLennan, G. (1995) *Pluralism*, Buckingham: Open University Press.

McNemar, Q. (1969) *Psychological Statistics*, 4th edn, New York: Wiley.

Mead, Margaret (1943) [1928] *Coming of Age in Samoa: A Study of Adolescence and Sex in Primitive Societies*, Harmondsworth: Penguin.

Melia, Kath M. (1996) 'Rediscovering Glaser', *Qualitative Health Research*, 6, 3, 368–78.

Menard, Scott (1991) *Longitudinal Research*, London: Sage.

Merton, R. K. and Kendall, P. L. (1946) 'The focused interview', *American Journal of Sociology*, 51, 541–57

Merton, R. K., Fiske, M. and Kendall, P. L. (1956) *The Focused Interview: A Manual of Problems and Procedures*, Glencoe, IL: Free Press.

Miller, W., Clarke, H., Harrop, M., Leduc, L. and Whiteley, P. (1990) *How Voters Change: The 1987 British Election Campaign in Perspective*, Oxford: Clarendon Press.

Mishler, Elliot G. (1986) *Research Interviewing: Context and Narrative*, Cambridge, MA: Harvard University Press.

Moorhouse, H. F. (1989) ' "We're off to Wembley": the history of a Scottish event and the sociology of football hooliganism', in D. McCrone, S. Kendrick and P. Straw (eds) *The Making of Scotland*, Edinburgh: Edinburgh University Press, 207–27.

Morgan, David L. (1997) *Focus Groups as Qualitative Research*, London: Sage.

Moser, C. and Kalton, G. (1985) *Survey Methods in Social Investigation*, 2nd edn, Aldershot: Gower.

Munn, P. and Drever, E. (1990) *Using Questionnaires in Small-Scale Research*, Edinburgh: Scottish Council for Research in Education.

Neave, G. (1998) 'Growing pains: the Dearing Report from a European perspective', *Higher Education Quarterly*, 52, 1, 118–36.

Oakes, J., Gamoran, A. and Page, R. N. (1992) 'Curriculum differentiation: opportunities, outcomes and meanings', in P. W. Jackson (ed.) *Handbook of Research on Curriculum*, New York: Macmillan, 570–608.

Oakley, A. (1981) 'Interviewing women: a contradiction in terms', in H. Roberts (ed.) *Doing Feminist Research*, London: Routledge and Kegan Paul, 30–61.

Oakley, A. and Fullerton, D. (1996) 'The lamp-post of research: support or illumination?', in A. Oakley and H. Roberts (eds) *Evaluating Social Interventions*, Ilford: Barnardo's, 4–38.

Oakley, A. and Roberts, H. (eds) (1996) *Evaluating Social Interventions*, Ilford: Barnardo's.

O'Muircheartaigh, I. and Lynn, P. (1997) 'The 1997 UK pre-election polls', *Journal of the Royal Statistical Society*, series A, 160, 3, 381–4.

Parry, G., Moyser, G. and Day, N. (1992) *Political Participation and Democracy in Britain*, Cambridge: Cambridge University Press.

Paterson, L. (1993) 'Local variation in the Scottish pilot projects of the Technical and Vocational Education Initiative', *Research Papers in Education*, 8, 1, 47–71.

Payne, S. L. (1951) *The Art of Asking Questions*, Princeton: Princeton University Press.

Platt, J. (1976) *Realities of Sociological Research*, Brighton: Sussex University Press.

Plummer, Ken (1983) *Documents of Life*, London: Allen and Unwin.

Pryke, Richard (1995) *Taking the Measure of Poverty*, London: Institute of Economic Affairs.

Raffe, D. (1987) 'The context of the Youth Training Scheme: an analysis of its strategy and development', *British Journal of Education and Work*, 1, 1, 1–31.

Raffe, D. (ed.) (1988) *Education and the Youth Labour Market*, London: Falmer.

Ragin, C. C. and Becker, H. S. (1992) *What is a Case?*, Cambridge: Cambridge University Press.

Rein, M. and Schon, D. A. (1977) 'Problem setting in policy research', in C. Weiss (ed.) *Using Social Research in Public Policy Making*, Lexington: Lexington Books, 235–51.

Reinharz, S. (1992) *Feminist Methods in Social Research*, Oxford: Oxford University Press.

Reynolds, D., Sammons, P., Stoll, L., Barber, M. and Hillman, J. (1996) 'School effectiveness and school improvement in the United Kingdom', *School Effectiveness and School Improvement*, 7, 2, 133–58.

Robertson, C. (1993) 'Participation in post-compulsory education in Scotland', *Journal of the Royal Statistical Society*, series A, 156, 3, 423–42.

Rowntree, B. S. (1901) *Poverty: A Study of Town Life*, London: Longmans, Green.

Runciman, W. G. (1966) *Relative Deprivation and Social Justice: A Study of Attitudes to Social Inequality in Twentieth Century England*, London: Routledge and Kegan Paul.

Rutter, M. (1989) 'Age as an ambiguous variable in developmental research: some epidemiological considerations from developmental psychopathology', *International Journal of Behavioral Development*, 12, 1, 1–34.

Sabatier, P. (1986) 'Top-down and bottom-up approaches to implementation research: a critical analysis and suggested synthesis', *Journal of Public Policy*, 6, 1, 21–48.

Said, E. (1993) *Culture and Imperialism*, London: Chatto and Windus.

Schuman, H. and Presser, S. (1981) *Questions and Answers in Attitude Surveys*, New York: Academic Press.

Scott, J. (1990) *A Matter of Record: Documentary Sources in Social Research*, Cambridge: Polity.

Scottish Office (1996) *Achievement for All*, Edinburgh: The Stationery Office.

SCPR (1996a) *Self Completion Questionnaires*, Survey Methods Centre Newsletter, 16, 1, London: Social and Community Planning Research.

——(1996b) *Using a Cognitive Perspective to Improve Questionnaire Design*, Survey Methods Centre Newsletter, 16, 2, London: Social and Community Planning Research.

Shaw, Clifford (1930) *The Jack-Roller*, Chicago: University of Chicago Press.

Sheridan, Dorothy (1993) 'Writing to the archive: mass-observation as autobiography', *Sociology*, 27, 1, 27–40.

Skinner, C. J., Holt, D. and Smith, T. M. F. (1989) *Analysis of Complex Surveys*, Chichester: Wiley.

Smith, D. E. (1987) *The Everyday World as Problematic: A Feminist Sociology*, Boston, MA: Northeastern University Press.

Smith, Lois M. (1994) 'Biographical method', in N. K. Denzin and Y. S. Lincoln (eds) *Handbook of Qualitative Research*, London: Sage, 286–305.

Smith, T. M. F. (1976) 'The foundations of survey sampling: a review', *Journal of the Royal Statistical Society*, A139, 2, 183–204.

——(1983) 'On the validity of inferences from non-random samples', *Journal of the Royal Statistical Society*, A146, 4, 394–403.

Sobel, Dava (1996) *Longitude*, London: Fourth Estate.

Spradley, J. P. (1979) *The Ethnographic Interview*, New York: Holt, Rinehart and Winston.

——(1980) *Participant Observation*, New York: Holt, Rinehart and Winston.

Stake, Robert E. (1994) 'Case studies', in N. K. Denzin and Y. S. Lincoln (eds) *Handbook of Qualitative Research*, London: Sage, 236–47.

Stewart, David W. (1990) *Focus Groups: Theory and Practice*, London: Sage.

Stitt, S. (1994) *Poverty and Poor Relief: Concepts and Reality*, Aldershot: Avebury.

Stitt, S. and Grant, D. (1993) *Poverty: Rowntree Revisited*, Aldershot: Avebury.

Stouffer, S. A. (1950) 'Some observations on study design', *American Journal of Sociology*, 85, 355–61.

Sykes, W. and Morton-Williams, J. (1987) 'Evaluating survey questions', *Journal of Official Statistics*, 3, 2, 191–207.

Thomas, W. I. and Znaniecki, F. (1958) *The Polish Peasant in Europe and America*, 2nd edn, London: Constable.

Thompson, Paul (1978) *The Voice of the Past: Oral History*, Oxford: Oxford University Press.

Timmins, N. (1996) *The Five Giants: A Biography of the Welfare State*, London: Fontana.

Tolstoy, L. (1957) [1863–9] *War and Peace*, trans. Rosemary Edmonds, Harmondsworth: Penguin Classics.

Tomlinson, T. M. (1990) 'Class size and public policy: the plot thickens', *Contemporary Education*, 62, 17–23.

Tooley, J. and Darby, D. (1998) *Educational Research: A Critique*, London: Ofsted.

Townsend, P. (1979) *Poverty in the United Kingdom: A Survey of Household Resources and Standards of Living*, Harmondsworth: Penguin.

Townsend, P. and Davidson, N. (1988) *Inequalities in Health*, Harmondsworth: Penguin.

Trow, M. (1998) 'The Dearing Report: a transatlantic view', *Higher Education Quarterly*, 52, 1, 93–117.

van Maanen, J. (1988) *Tales of the Field: On Writing Ethnography*, Chicago: University of Chicago Press.

Wagenaar, H. C., Kallen, D. B. P. and Kosse, G. B. (1982) 'Social science and public policy making in the 1980s', in D. B. P. Kallen, G. B. Kosse, H. C. Wagenaar, J. J. J. Kloprogge and M. Vorbeck (eds) *Social Science Research and Public Policy Making*, Windsor: NFER-Nelson, 7–20.

Wainwright, H. (1994) *Arguments for a New Left*, Oxford: Blackwell.

Walden, R. and Walkerdine, V. (1985) *Girls and Mathematics*, London: Institute of Education.

Walford, G. (1988) 'Shouts of joy and cries of pain: investigating young people's comments on leaving school and entering the labour market', in D. Raffe (ed.) *Education and the Youth Labour Market*, London: Falmer, 243–65.

Webb, E., Campbell, D. T., Schwarz, R. C. and Sechrest, L. (1966) *Unobtrusive Measures: Nonreactive Research in the Social Sciences*, Chicago: Rand McNally.

Weiss, C. (1977b) 'Introduction', in C. Weiss (ed.) *Using Social Research in Public Policy Making*, Lexington: Lexington Books, 1–22.

——(1982) 'Policy research in the context of diffuse decision making', in D. B. P. Kallen, G. B. Kosse, H. C. Wagenaar, J. J. J. Kloprogge and M. Vorbeck (eds) *Social Science Research and Public Policy Making*, Windsor: NFER-Nelson, 288–305.

——(1986) 'The many meanings of research utilisation', in M. Bulmer (ed.) *Social Science and Social Policy*, London: Allen and Unwin, 31–40.

Weiss, C. (ed.) (1977a) *Using Social Research in Public Policy Making*, Lexington: Lexington Books.

Whyte, William Foote (1955) *Street Corner Society: The Social Structure of an Italian Slum*, 2nd edn, Chicago: University of Chicago Press.

Willer, D. and Willer, J. (1973) *Systematic Empiricism: Critique of a Pseudo-Science*, Englewood Cliffs: Prentice-Hall.

Willms, J. D. (1992) *Monitoring School Performance*, London: Falmer.

Yin, Robert K. (1993) *Applications of Case Study Research*, Newbury Park, CA: Sage.

——(1994) *Case Study Research: Design and Methods*, revised edn, Beverley Hills: Sage.
Young, M. (1965) *Innovation and Research in Education*, London: Routledge and Kegan Paul.

Index